Co-producing SMAI Targets for Childrer with SEND

T0372254

This accessible guide supports school and education settings in co-producing SMART targets for education health and care plans, SEN support plans and Personal Education Plans.

The book encourages educators to collaborate with children, young people and their caregivers to gain an in-depth understanding of their views, aspirations, strengths and areas of challenge, and to write purposeful, specific, measurable and achievable targets. Each chapter offers successful approaches to capture authentic voice, with a variety of contributors sharing their journey to improve child and family leadership by developing child-centred approaches in their contexts. The book includes case studies and reflective activities to further support the reader with creative and innovative approaches to SMART targets that are underpinned by the child's perspective.

With contributions from a range of schools, and across age phases, this book encourages and enables collaboration with children, young people and their caregivers, and will be essential reading for SENCOs, designated leads for safeguarding, teachers and senior leaders in both mainstream and specialist settings.

Sarah Martin-Denham is Senior Lecturer at the University of Sunderland and Programme Leader for the National Award for Special Educational Needs Coordination on-campus route. In addition, she leads externally funded research for a range of organisations on school exclusion, childhood adversities and service evaluations in children's social care. Sarah's passion for child and caregiver voice comes from her experiences as a mother and teacher. This book forms part of Sarah's ambition to ensure children and their caregivers are given agency in decisions regarding their education and care.

Co-producing SMART Targets for Children with SEND

Capturing the Authentic Voice of Children, Young People and their Caregivers

Edited by
Sarah Martin-Denham

Routledge
Taylor & Francis Group

LONDON AND NEW YORK

Cover image: Getty

First published 2023
by Routledge
4 Park Square, Milton Park, Abingdon, Oxon OX14 4RN

and by Routledge
605 Third Avenue, New York, NY 10158

Routledge is an imprint of the Taylor & Francis Group, an informa business

British Library Cataloguing-in-Publication Data
A catalogue record for this book is available from the British Library

Library of Congress Cataloging-in-Publication Data
A catalog record for this book has been requested

ISBN: 978-1-032-19933-7 (hbk)
ISBN: 978-1-032-19931-3 (pbk)
ISBN: 978-1-003-26150-6 (ebk)

DOI: 10.4324/9781003261506

Typeset in Optima
by Apex CoVantage, LLC

Contents

CONTENTS

Contributors

Johanna Butler

Johanna is a trained speech and language therapist. She now works full-time at Hopespring Charity, after having volunteered for the charity since 2013 while working for the NHS in an adult autism team and secure mental health hospital. Johanna is passionate about ensuring every young person's needs are met and their voices are heard to enable them to access education. She was invited by Hopespring to train both as a teacher then as a SENCO and currently practises in a dual role across Hopespring schools.

Dominick Gray

Dominick has over 17 years of experience supporting young people within alternative provisions in the North East. He is currently Head Teacher and SENCO at a Pupil Referral Unit in South Tyneside, supporting students across key stages 1 to 4. One of his key priorities is to ensure young people with social, emotional and mental health issues are fully supported within mainstream education and given extensive opportunities to develop their coping strategies and resilience. Dominick has developed his interest in Adverse Childhood Experiences and strives to improve staff understanding by utilising assessment tools to effectively support young people.

Danny Kilkenny

Danny has taught in a secondary mainstream provision for 20 years. He has been Department Leader for History, has been Assistant Principal in Teaching and Learning, and is currently Vice Principal of Curriculum. Last year, he completed his NASENCO qualification at the

University of Sunderland. With his background in teaching and learning, Danny is keen to raise the profile of learners with SEN in mainstream class-rooms and offer teachers support and professional development to ensure that quality first teaching is the norm.

Catherine Landucci

Catherine is an experienced SENCO, SEN teacher and foster carer based in North London. Having worked in various schools with contrasting demo-graphics, she has a good understanding of the realities of providing for and teaching children with SEND in mainstream primary schools. Through her fostering role, she has more recently experienced what it is like to navigate and advocate from the other side of the playground. Catherine has devel-oped particular interests and expertise in trauma-informed practice and solution-focused provision and support for children with SEN.

Peter Monaghan

Peter is Curriculum Leader and Governor in further education and has a range of experience, including teaching in secondary schools, higher edu-cation and the voluntary sector. He is a PhD candidate in education and social justice, particularly interested in inclusive practices outside of com-pulsory education. Peter is a member of the national FE practitioner advi-sory group (PAG) for the Society for Education and Training.

Jane Pickthall

Jane is the Virtual School Head for North Tyneside Council and has sup-ported care-experienced children and young people for over 20 years. The Virtual School sits within a multi-agency team including nurses, teachers and therapeutic practitioners. Jane also manages North Tyneside's Bar-nardo's Alliance and the Mental Health Support Team for schools, focusing on early help and prevention to improve emotional wellbeing. Jane was a founding trustee of the National Association of Virtual School Heads and sat on the board until March 2021, having been Chair and Honorary Treas-urer. Jane was awarded an MBE in 2021.

Denise Taylor

Denise is Principal at Beacon School of Light. Following a career in sec-ondary mainstream education, spanning over 20 years in Sunderland and

Gateshead, Denise returned to Sunderland in 2015, establishing the Beacon of Light School. Working with a wide range of 13–16-year-olds across the Northeast 'on the margins of mainstream', the school embeds a strong foundation for all to thrive as individuals, to believe in their abilities fully and to secure the future success they deserve.

Dr Wendy Thorley

Wendy is retired Academic, Director of Children's Emotional Language and Thinking and Director of ACE Network North East. She completed her PhD, master's degree and BA (Hons) in Education following her Registered General Nurse training and career. Wendy originally worked in health before moving to primary education, further education then higher education. She was awarded the National Fellowship for teaching by the Higher Education Academy in 2013.

Donna Walker

Donna is Headteacher at the Link School Sunderland. She has been teaching for over 20 years and started her career working in a mainstream school. Donna's move into alternative provision has changed her educational focus and deepened her commitment to making a real difference in helping young people gain the necessary skills to succeed throughout their school career and beyond.

Faye Waterhouse

Faye is Assistant Headteacher at Walkergate Community School. She is a qualified SENCO and a Specialist Leader of Education (SLE). She has a master's in Education specialising in Early Years. Faye has a passion for early years and is dedicated to developing teaching and learning for all children and their families. She has 11 years' experience of teaching in schools alongside leading others to develop best practices to meet all children's needs.

Kerrie Whelan

Kerrie is Headteacher at Endeavour Academy. She has over 20 years' experience working with young people who have disengaged from education. Her passion for promoting positive mental health was evident in the partnerships she developed to establish a large network of mental health champions. Kerrie strives to provide a safe and nurturing environment for young people with a focus on resilience to become successful and confident learners and responsible citizens in their communities.

Acknowledgements

Special thanks to my family, Ben, Emily and William, for giving me the time and support to be the editor of this book. As always, thanks to my sister Lucy for giving me the confidence to do this work and my dad for telling me to just get on with it. Thanks to my students past and present for the learning we do together day after day. This book has been produced in partnership with members of the University of Sunderland Independent SENCO Network. Thank you to the contributors for your chapters and the time you have taken to share your experiences – to do this during a global pandemic is incredible. You all amaze me with the work you do, day after day, to support children and their families. Also, thanks to Nathan Scott – you have been by my side as a research assistant since February 2021 and worked tirelessly to support my many projects. Thank you to you all.

The review of this book was funded by UKRI Policy Support Fund 2021–2022, awarded to the University of Sunderland.

Abbreviations

ACE	adverse childhood experience
ACL	adult and community learning
ADHD	attention deficit hyperactivity disorder
AP	alternative provision
BSP	behaviour support plan
CAFA	Children and Families Act (2014)
CAMHS	Child and Adolescent Mental Health Services
CCVAB	childhood challenging, violent or aggressive behaviour
CiC	children in care
CiN	children in need
CPD	continuous professional development
CYP	children and young people
DCSF	Department for Children, Schools and Families
DfE	Department for Education
DfES	Department for Education and Skills
DoH	Department of Health
EHCP	education, health and care plan
EYFS	Early Years Foundation Stage
FASD	foetal alcohol spectrum disorders
FE	further education
FSM	free school meals
GCSE	General Certificate of Secondary Education
HLTA	higher level teaching assistant
IAG	information, advice and guidance
IEP	individual education plan
IPSEA	Independent Provider of Special Education Advice
LA	local authority

LAC	looked after children
LACES	Looked After Children Education Services
LDD	learning difficulties and disabilities
LO	learning objective
LSA	learning support assistant
LSS	Learning Support Services
NCER	National Center for Education Research
NE	North East
Ofsted	Office for Standards in Education
PECS	picture exchange communication system
PEP	Personal Education Plan
PRU	Pupil Referral Unit
QFT	quality first teaching
SDQ	Strengths and Difficulties Questionnaire
SEMH	social, emotional and mental health
SEN	special educational needs
SEND	special educational needs and/or disabilities
SENCO	special educational needs coordinator
SEP	special educational provision
SLCN	speech, language and communication needs
SMART	specific, measurable, achievable, relevant and time-bound
UK	United Kingdom
UNCRC	United Nations Convention on the Rights of the Child
VSH	virtual school headteacher
YDAP	Youth, Drug and Alcohol Project

Glossary of terms

Active listening: Focusing entirely on what the child is saying and understanding the emotions and feelings underlying the message

Alternative provision: For children of compulsory school age who do not attend mainstream or special schools

Care pathway: The route a person takes through health care services

Child Protection Plan: A plan drawn up by social care services to protect a child who they feel is suffering or is likely to suffer significant harm

Children in need: Children within social care services who do not meet the threshold for being 'looked after' but are receiving intervention from social care services

Designated teachers: Champions the educational attainment of looked after and permanently placed children

Early Years Foundation Stage: The framework for the learning, development and care of children from birth to five years

Education Health and Care Plan: Details the education, health and social care support that is to be provided to a child with SEN and/or disabilities

Graduated response: A model of action and intervention to support children who have SEN

Local authority (LA): A body responsible for a range of vital services for people and businesses in defined areas

Local offer: LA information about provision they expect to be available across education, health and social care for children in their area who have SEND

Maintained school: Schools which a LA maintains

Manipulatives: An object that supports a child to learn concepts through hands-on experience

NHS England: An independent body that improves health outcomes for people in England

Ofsted: Responsible for the inspection of all schools in England

Pupil Referral Unit: Provides education for children who would otherwise not receive suitable education because of illness, exclusion or any other reason

Special educational needs (SEN): A child has SEN if they have a learning difficulty or disability that calls for special educational provision to be made

Special educational needs coordinator (SENCO): A qualified teacher in a school or maintained nursery school who has responsibility for coordinating SEN provision

Social care: All forms of personal care and other practical assistance for children who need extra support

Special educational provision: Provision that is different from or additional to that which is universally available to children with SEN to enable them to access and participate in learning

Specialist school: A school that is specifically organised to make special educational provisions for children with SEN

Stakeholder: An organisation/individual with interest in a topic, including public sector providers and commissioners of care or services

Statutory duty: A duty that must be complied with

Young person: A person over compulsory school age (the end of the academic year in which they turn 16) to the age of 25

Introduction

I am delighted to welcome this book, *Co-producing SMART targets for children with SEND: capturing the authentic voice of children, young people and their caregivers*, to the Routledge collection.

The book has been created with the most inspirational people I have ever met. Over the years, you gravitate towards those with whom you have commonality, and through this, our partnership has thrived and grown. The writers share an ethos of enabling, building and sustaining connections and relationships with children and their caregivers. Through this, trust, safety, a sense of belonging and participation are gained.

In the eight years that I have trained SENCOs for their National Award for Special Educational Needs Coordination, I am yet to meet one who is confident in their or their colleagues' ability to co-produce and create high-quality SMART targets. To be effective, targets need to be based on children's and caregivers' wishes, views and feelings; they should underpin provision and practice. The means by which 'voice' is captured and embedded in the care and education of children and young people (CYP) varies across provisions. This book is designed and structured to support you wherever you are on the journey. The move towards an ethos of genuine co-production takes time, investment and training. The outcome of co-production is stronger relationships and connections with CYP and their caregivers. Enjoy the journey.

As you read this book, you may feel that your setting is at the very start of the journey. Please know that many nurseries, schools

DOI: 10.4324/9781003261506-1

and colleges feel this way. There are multiple barriers to capturing CYP and caregiver 'voices'; some of which you may recognise:

- School staff have always decided and written targets 'on behalf' of children and their caregivers.
- School systems and processes do not involve child and caregiver voices.
- Training on co-producing provision and practice are not available.
- It isn't a priority.
- Time is lacking for teachers to meet with CYP and caregivers.
- Inability to find or create a suitable design and structure to capture, record and respond to voice.
- Supporting caregivers who are reluctant to participate due to their own negative experiences of schooling or interactions with schools as adults.
- Others simply do not know where to start. They are not alone.

Support plans for children with special educational needs (SEN) have been described as vague and shallow (Gallagher and Desimone, 1995; Ruble et al., 2010; Sanches-Ferreira et al., 2013; Martin-Denham, 2020). Many targets are neither measurable nor achievable, nor related to the strengths and needs of children with SEND (Martin-Denham and Watts, 2019). Research has highlighted that the most significant improvement areas in writing targets are measurability (Ruble et al., 2010; Sanches-Ferreira et al., 2013) and functionality (Boavida et al., 2010).

Through reading the chapters in this book, you will be able to identify what your setting needs to develop and prioritise. The book sets out training activities, provides useful proformas and showcases good practice to guide you in transforming how you embed the voice of CYP into co-creating SMART targets and provision and practice within your organisations.

All CYP's names have been changed throughout this book to protect their identity. *CYP* refers to children and young people from 0 to 25 years. *Caregivers* refer to any person with parental responsibility (including kinship carers and foster carers).

This is a not-for-profit book. The editor has donated all royalties to Durham Dales Hockey Club to support their outreach work in the North of England for CYP with SEND.

References

Boavida, T., Aguiar, C., McWilliam, R.A. and Pimentel, J.S. (2010) 'Quality of individualized education program goals of pre-schoolers with disabilities', *Infants and Young Children*, 23(3), pp. 233–243.

Gallagher, J. and Desimone, L. (1995) 'Lessons learned from the implementation of the IEP. Applications to the IFSP', *Topics in Early Special Education*, 15(3), pp. 353–379.

Martin-Denham, S. (2020) *The enablers and barriers to mainstream schooling: The voices of children excluded from school, their caregivers, and professionals.* Sunderland: University of Sunderland.

Martin-Denham, S. and Watts, S. (2019) *SENCO handbook: Leading provision and practice.* London: SAGE Publications, Ltd.

Ruble, L.A., McGrew, J., Dalrymple, N. and Jung, L.A. (2010) 'Examining the quality of IEPs for young children with autism', *Journal of Autism and Developmental Disorders*, 40(12), pp. 1459–1470.

Sanches-Ferreira, M., Lopes-dos-Santos, P., Alves, S., Santos, M. and Silveira-Maia, M. (2013) 'How individualised are the Individualised Education Programmes (IEPs): An analysis of the contents and quality of the IEPs goals', *European Journal of Special Needs Education*, 28, pp. 507–520.

Co-production

1

The legal and regulatory context and the role of continuous professional development (CPD)

Sarah Martin-Denham

This chapter provides an overview of relevant legislation, convention and policy regarding person-centred approaches to creating plans for children with special educational needs and disabilities (SEND). The chapter provides the basis for supporting colleagues within settings through dedicated continuous professional development (CPD) activities. It includes a step-by-step guide to developing understanding and confidence in writing SMART targets that incorporate the voices of CYP and their caregivers as something that are devised with rather than for them. Before commencing the CPD sessions, read Chapter 2 to ensure any targets formed are co-produced with CYP and their caregiver to encapsulate their views, wishes and feelings.

The Children and Families Act 2014

The Children and Families Act (CAFA) 2014 Part 3 is the most recent statute law that brings together previous legislation. The CAFA (2014) has attempted to mandate the importance of listening to and hearing the voice of CYP, obliging education providers to work in partnership with children and their families to identify learning outcomes and to plan special education provision (SEP).

The CAFA (2014) sought to commit the government to support three key groups of children:

DOI: 10.4324/9781003261506-2

- Those in the adoption and care system (part 1)
- Those affected by family courts (part 2)
- Those with SEND (part 3)

The United Nations Convention on the Rights of the Child

The United Nations Convention on the Rights of the Child (UNCRC) (UNICEF, 1989) article 12 established the right for children to freely express their views in matters affecting them, giving their views due weight according to their age and maturity.

Article 12 of the UNCRC states this:

1 States Parties shall assure to the child who is capable of forming his or her own views the right to express those views freely in all matters affecting the child, the views of the child being given due weight in accordance with the age and maturity of the child.
2 For this purpose, the child shall in particular be provided the opportunity to be heard in any judicial and administrative proceedings affecting the child, the views of the child being given due weight in accordance with the age and maturity of the child.

(UNICEF, 1989. p. 5)

The principles underpinning the special educational needs and disability (SEND) code of practice (Department for Education (DfE) and Department of Health (DoH), 2015, p. 19) are designed to support 'the participation of children, their caregivers and young people in decision making'.

Definitions of special educational needs and disability

- A CYP has SEN if they have a learning difficulty or disability that calls for special educational provision to be made for him or her.

- A child of compulsory school age or older has a learning difficulty or disability if he/she has the following:
  1. A significantly greater difficulty in learning than the majority of others of the same age
  2. A disability that causes hindrance from making use of educational facilities generally provided in mainstream schools or post-16 institutions

Many CYP who have SEN may have a disability under the Equality Act (2010), defined as 'a physical or mental impairment which has a long term and substantial adverse effect on their ability to carry out normal day-to-day activities'. The Equality Act (2010) replaced nine acts of parliament and hundreds of regulations to provide a single consolidated source of discrimination law. The act makes it unlawful for the responsible body of a school to discriminate against, harass or victimise a pupil or potential pupil:

- In relation to admissions
- In the way it provides education for pupils
- In the way it provides pupils access to any benefit, facility or service, or
- By excluding a pupil or subjecting them to any other detriment

(DfE, 2014, p. 7)

The CAFA 2014 intensified previous statutory requirements to involve parents in decisions directly affecting children with SEND. The reforms to SEND were partly due to the need to increase parental confidence in the SEN system. It was the Lamb Inquiry (Department for Children, Schools and Families (DCSF), 2009, p. 3) that reported this:

> In the most successful schools, the effective engagement of parents has had a profound impact on children's progress and the confidence between the school and parent. Parents need to be listened to more and brought into a partnership with statutory bodies in a more meaningful way.

From the CAFA (2014) to the DfE and DoH (2015) Code, the emphasis on support for parents in early identification (of SEND), high-quality provision, decision-making, choice and control, and collaboration between agencies was clear. Despite this, the House of Commons Education Committee (2018, p. 3) expressed failures in implementing the CAFA (2014), leading to 'unlawful practice, bureaucratic nightmares, buck-passing, lack of accountability, strained resources and adversarial experiences'.

The convention emphasised a child's right to be listened to and heard in decisions affecting them. The legislative duties afforded to CYP and their caregivers relate somewhat to the UNICEF (1989), ratified in 1991 by the United Kingdom (UK) government and the duties afforded children and families in the Children Act 1989, CAFA (2014) and Equality Act 2010. The articles within the UNICEF (1989) are enacted in the CAFA (2014) and the statutory DfE and DoH (2015) SEND code of practice (Table 1.1). The CAFA

Table 1.1 The correlation between UNICEF (1989), CAFA (2014) and DfE and DoH (2015)

UNCRC (1989)	CAFA (2014)	DfE and DoH (2015) SEND code of practice
Every child has the right to express their views, feelings and wishes in all matters affecting them and to have their views considered and taken seriously (article 12)	**(a) the views, wishes and feelings of the child and his or her parent, or the young person**	The principles of the code of practice (p. 19) Special educational provision in schools (p. 99) Duties on Local Authorities (p. 123) Transition assessments for young people with EHCPs (p. 137) Considering whether an EHC needs assessment is necessary (p. 145) Involving children, young people and parents in decision-making (p. 147–148) Advice and information for EHC needs assessments (p. 155) Requests for a particular school, college or other institution (p. 173–174) Reviewing an EHC plan (p. 194) Preparing for adulthood in reviews (p. 200) SEN and social care needs, including children in need (p. 214–215) Advice and information for an assessment of post-detention education, health and care needs (p. 229)

(Continued)

Table 1.1 (Continued) The correlation between UNICEF (1989), CAFA (2014) and DfE and DoH (2015

UNCRC (1989)	CAFA (2014)	DfE and DoH (2015) SEND code of practice
Every child must be free to express their thoughts and opinions and to access all kinds of information, as long as it is within the law (article 13)	**(b) the importance of the child and his or her parent, or the young person, participating as fully as possible in decisions relating to the exercise of the function concerned**	The principles underpinning the code of practice (p. 19) The principles in practice (p. 20) Referenced throughout the Code
Governments must respect the rights and responsibilities of parents and carers to provide guidance and direction to their child as they grow up so that they fully enjoy their rights. This must be done in a way that recognises the child's increasing capacity to make their own choices (article 5) Every child must be free to express their thoughts and opinions and to access all kinds of information (article 13)	**(c) the importance of the child and his or her parent, or the young person, being provided with the information and support necessary to enable participation in those decisions**	The principles underpinning the code of practice (p. 19) Supporting children, young people and parents to participate in decisions about their support (p. 21) Impartial information, advice and support (p. 30) What needs to be provided? (p. 33)
The best interests of the child must be a top priority in all decisions and actions that affect children (article 3) A child with a disability has the right to live a full and decent life with dignity and, as far as possible, independence, and to	**(d) the need to support the child and his or her parent, or the young person, in order to facilitate the development of the child or young person and to help him or her achieve the best possible educational and other outcomes**	The principles in practice (p. 21) The Mental Capacity Act (p. 128) Support for children, young people and parents (p. 150) Outcomes (p. 163) Use of direct payments (p. 184) Children with SEN who are in alternative provision (p. 216)

UNCRC (1989)	CAFA (2014)	DfE and DoH (2015) SEND code of practice
play an active part in the community (article 23) Education must develop every child's personality, talents and abilities to the full (article 29)		

(UNICEF, 1989; CAFA, 2014, s.19; DfE and DoH, 2015)

(2014) is explicit that LA functions in England in supporting and involving CYP must have regard to the following:

a   The views, wishes and feelings of the child and his or her parent, or the young person
b   The importance of the child and his or her parent, or the young person, participating as fully as possible in decisions relating to the exercise of the function concerned
c   The importance of the child and his or her parent, or the young person, being provided with the information and support necessary to enable participation in those decisions
d   The need to support the child and his or her parent, or the young person, in order to facilitate the development of the child or young person and to help him or her achieve the best possible educational and other outcomes

(CAFA, 2014, s.19)

Involving caregivers

Historically, the UK strategy had fundamental principles stating the importance of involving caregivers in decision-making in the SEN code of practice (DfE and DoH, 2015; DfE, 1994). The momentum continued in the Department for Education and Skills (DfES) (2001) SEN code.

> The knowledge, views and experience of parents are vital. Effective assessment and provision will be secured where there is the greatest possible degree of

partnership between parents and their children and schools, LEAs and other agencies.

(DfE, 1994, p. 13)

Parents have a vital role to play in supporting their child's education

(DfES, 2001, p. 7)

There are, of course, challenges with forming effective partnerships with caregivers. First, there needs to be a willingness to involve CYP in decisions regarding their education (Partridge, 2005). Second, as the Driver Youth Trust (2015, p. 45) suggested, 'communicating with parents can be difficult, particularly when there are differences in understanding a child's needs or limited knowledge of the difficulties on either side'. It is widely understood that the greater the level of caregiver engagement, the better outcomes, progression and attainment for children (Desforges and Abouchaar, 2003; Goodall and Vorhaus, 2011). Brokenbrow, Horridge and Stair (2016) captured the views of 10 young people and 123 carers of children with disabilities, and noted the importance of acknowledging the role of caregivers. 'Take the time to listen to what the person and those who know them best say that they need, with the patience to understand that some barriers to inclusion may be hidden' (p. 8).

Involving children

It was only the 2001 (DfES) SEN Code that included the fundamental principle of child voice: 'the views of the child should be sought and taken into account' (p. 7). However, in other sections of the 1994 Code, p. 26, schools were asked to consider how they do the following:

- Involve pupils in decision-making processes
- Determine the pupil's level of participation, taking into account approaches to assessment and intervention which are suitable for his or her age, ability and past experiences
- Record pupils' views on identifying their difficulties, setting goals, agreeing on a development strategy, monitoring and reviewing progress
- Involve pupils in implementing individual education plans (IEPs)

'He said that a lot of it was because he couldn't do the work. He said he told them that the work was too hard and that he needed to go into a different group or something like that. But the school said it was because he wanted to be with his friends.'

Figure 1.1 Caregiver comment
(Martin-Denham, 2020a, p. 11)

Sadly, research has shown that the rhetoric in legislation and policy was not reflected in educational practice. Sales and Vincent (2018) described how the teachers in their study acknowledged that listening to CYP felt tokenistic. Likewise, Merrick (2020) identified that 84% of teachers from an online survey (N=64) indicated that they would like more involvement from CYP about decisions about their provision. They added that the barrier to their participation is the nature of their difficulties and negative teacher attitudes.

Despite the legislation, convention and policy, there are inconsistencies in how well CYP are listened to and heard, and how their voices are acted upon (Martin-Denham, 2020a, 2020b, 2020c, 2020d, 2021, 2022). The Martin-Denham research on school exclusion and social, emotional and mental health needs (2020–2022) illustrated that children and caregivers want to be listened to; they know their challenges with participating in schooling (Figure 1.1).

Other research indicates that inclusive methods that capture the views of all stakeholders, including children, are most effective in supporting wellbeing and positive academic outcomes (Doyle, 1986; Emmer and Stough, 2001; Gillett-Swan, 2013, 2014).

Education, health and care plans

Securing parental engagement is woven into legislation as part of the CAFA (2014). The purpose of the education, health and care plan (EHCP) is 'to make special educational provision to meet the special educational needs of the child or young person, to secure the best possible outcomes for them across education, health and social care and, as they get older, prepare them for adulthood' (DfE and DoH, 2015, p. 142). The Independent Provider of Special Education Advice (IPSEA) (2021) notes that if a LA is requested to carry out an EHC needs assessment, they must consider the following:

- Whether the CYP has or may have SEN
- Whether special educational provision may be required (EHCP)

The CAFA (2014) established a legal obligation to assess needs where the previous criteria are met.

The reality is somewhat different to the policy ideology, with financial pressures on schools contributing to their unwillingness to identify children's challenges and provide support (House of Commons, 2019). Martin-Denham (2022) identified that a key issue was some schools declining to support caregivers of children with autism with an application for an EHCP needs assessment, despite their child meeting the legal test: 'may have an SEN' (IPSEA, 2021). EHCPs have received widespread criticism for having a 'within-child' view of their support needs (Buck, 2015; Hunter et al., 2019) instead of a view based on a holistic understanding of the child and how they interact within the school environment.

- Professionals working with children during the EHC needs assessment and EHC plan development process may agree to shorter-term targets that are not part of the EHC plan. These can be reviewed and, if necessary, regularly amended to ensure that individual remains on track to achieve the outcomes specified in their EHC plan
- Professionals should, wherever possible, append these shorter-term plans and targets to the EHC plan so that regular progress monitoring is always considered in the light of longer-term outcomes and aspirations

(DfE and DoH, 2015, 9.69)

Review of EHCPs (9.166/9.167)

The review must do the following:

- Consider whether outcomes and supporting targets remain appropriate
- Set new interim targets for the coming year and, where appropriate, agree on new outcomes

- Review any interim targets set by the early years provider, school or college, or other education providers

SEN support plans and information systems

Usually, schools have an SEN support plan, historically known as an IEP. In addition, they will have an information system (typically called a provision map) that records and monitors the children's SEND, outcomes, support, teaching strategies, interventions and involvement of health, education and care specialists.

Part 3 of the 1993 Education Act sets out legal duties for local education authorities (LEAs), health services and social services on their responsibilities towards children with SEN. The act led to parliament approving the SEND code of practice on the Identification and Assessment of Special Educational Needs (DfE, 1994). The rhetoric was that the 1993 Education Act and the DfE (1994) guidance would mandate IEPs as the tool to bring together identification, provision and review for CYP with SEN. Many issues were identified with the 1994 code, including increased workload for SENCOs, due to the requirement for the review of IEPs three times a year alongside the annual review of statements of SEN (Office for Standards in Education (Ofsted), 1999; Gross, 2000). Ofsted (1999) concluded in their review of the 1994 Code that IEPs are redundant unless they are part of effective educational planning. The purpose of setting targets is to plan the support they will receive (Räty, Vehkakoski and Pirttimaa, 2019).

The code (DfE and DoH) (2015) clarifies what teachers should do:

> Use appropriate assessment to set targets which are deliberately ambitious. Potential areas of difficulty should be identified and addressed at the outset. Lessons should be planned to address potential areas of difficulty and to remove barriers to pupil achievement
>
> (p. 94)

> Readily share this information with parents in a format that is accessible (for example, a note setting out the areas of discussion following a regular SEN support meeting or tracking data showing the pupils progress together with

13

highlighted sections of a provision map that enables parents to see what support has been provided.

(DfE and DoH, 2015, p. 105)

Effective systems and processes for capturing, recording and monitoring targets and interventions enable the SENCO to maintain a strategic overview of the SEP on outcomes for individuals and groups of children across a school. The SENCO can determine which interventions have a positive impact and gaps, and which interventions to discontinue through provision management.

The purpose of SEN support plans

The graduated approach should be led by the SENCO, working with and supporting practitioners (DfE and DoH, 2015, p. 87), though 'teachers are responsible and accountable for the progress and development of pupils in their class, including where they access support from teaching assistants' (p. 99). Within the graduated approach, it is explicit (DfE and DoH, 2015, 5:40) 'once parents have been formally notified, the practitioner and SENCOs should agree, in consultation with the parent, the outcomes they are seeking, the interventions and support to be put in place, the expected impact on progress, development on behaviour, and a clear date for review'. Plans should consider the views of the child' (Early Years Foundation Stage (EYFS)).

- The support and intervention should be selected to meet outcomes identified for the child, based on reliable evidence of effectiveness provided by practitioners with relevant skills and knowledge
- Any related staff development needs should be identified and addressed
- Parents should be involved in planning support and where appropriate, in reinforcing the provision or contributing to progress at home

(DfE and DoH, 2015, pp. 86–87)

Review of SEN support plans

- Schools must provide an annual report to parents on their child's progress (most will want to go beyond), providing regular updates

- Schools should talk to parents frequently to set clear outcomes and review progress towards them, discuss activities and support that will help achieve them, and identify the responsibilities of the parent, pupil and school
- Schools should meet parents at least three times each year

(DfE and DoH, 2015, p. 104)

Early years providers, schools and colleges should know precisely where CYP with SEN are in their learning and development (1.25). They should do the following:

- Have high ambitions and set stretching targets for them
- Track their progress towards these goals
- Keep under review the additional or different provision that is made for them
- Promote positive outcomes in the wider areas of personal and social development
- Ensure that the approaches use the best possible evidence and are having the required impact on progress

 REFLECTIVE ACTIVITY

Read the SEN support plan (Table 1.2), then consider if this meets the requirements and spirit of the CAFA (2014), including the following:

a   The views, wishes and feelings of the child and his or her parent, or the young person
b   The importance of the child and his or her parent, or the young person, participating as fully as possible in decisions relating to the exercise of the function concerned
c   The importance of the child and his or her parent, or the young person, being provided with the information and support necessary to enable participation in those decisions
d   The need to support the child and his or her parent, or the young person, in order to facilitate the development of the CYP and to help him or her achieve the best possible educational and other outcomes

Table 1.2 Bertie's SEN support plan

Name: Bertie
Year group: 5
Attendance: 97%
Attainment: Expected level
Strengths: Good at sports   **Child's views:** I don't like some of my lessons
Challenges: Cognition   **Caregiver's views:** They agree with the plan
and learning: specific to
handwriting skills and
concentration

Agreed outcomes

Target	Intervention and frequency	Teacher	Resource	Outcome achieved Y/N/Partial
To develop concentration within a small group	Lego therapy Twice, 45 minutes a fortnight	Mrs New	Lego therapy	
To develop coping skills in school	One-to-one support for most literacy lessons	Mrs New	Teaching assistant	
To regulate anxiety	Counselling, as and when needed	Mrs New to support	Teaching assistant	

Finding out activity

Think about the current SEN support plans you are working to deliver for children or young people, specifically for the following (you will return to this activity later in the chapter, so please keep your answers as notes to look back on):

- Who decides the CYP's targets (for example, individual class teachers, support staff, subject leads, form tutors, pastoral team, SENCO, CYP or caregivers)
- How and when are targets decided (include how often)?
- Where does the information come from to inform the plan (for example, is it from those who set the targets or is this after the targets are set by one or two people)?

- Are targets co-produced with the CYP, caregiver, teacher and other agencies (make notes specifically on how co-production is performed. For example, is there a meeting prior to and during target setting, with an agreement reached in finalising the target)?
- Whom do you feel the plans are for (for example, are they mainly for the caregivers and children or someone else? If so, for whom)?
- Do the targets set directly and clearly link to the child's SEN as identified on their SEN register?
- How reflective are targets of the views, wishes and feelings of the CYP and their caregivers (provide detail of how this is known to the team)?
- How SMART do you think your targets are (for example, extremely good, good, mainly good or unsure)?

What are SMART targets?

SMART targets are a form of objective that allows you to track short- and long-term goals. To be effective, targets need to be specific, measurable, achievable, relevant and time-bound (SMART); otherwise, they will be neither observable nor measurable (Table 1.3). For SMART targets to be effective, they need to be developed in collaboration with the CYP and their caregivers, and underpinned by their views, wishes and feelings.

Table 1.3 SMART targets for CYP with SEND

Specific	What do you want them to be able to do?
	Are the targets related to their needs, interests, skills and stage in the learning process (their ability rather than chronological age)?
	Are the targets child-centred and based on their views, wishes and feelings?
	Is each target clear, precise, well-defined and unambiguous?
Measurable	How will you know they have achieved the target? What measure will you use?
	Can their success be observed?
	Can you give a yes/no response to 'have they achieved the target?'
Achievable	Is the target realistically achievable?
	What might affect or impact their ability to achieve the target?
	Is the target agreeable with the child and caregiver? Is it attainable?
	Are any required provisions/resources available to the child?

(Continued)

Table 1.3 (Continued) SMART targets for CYP with SEND

Specific	What do you want them to be able to do?
	Are the targets related to their needs, interests, skills and stage in the learning process (their ability rather than chronological age)?
	Are the targets child-centred and based on their views, wishes and feelings?
	Is each target clear, precise, well-defined and unambiguous?
Relevant	Is the target at the right level for the child?
	Why are you setting the target?
Time-Bound	When should they be able to achieve the target?
	What are the start and end dates?
	When will their progress be reviewed?

Adapted from Martin-Denham and Watts (2019, p. 27)

Leading CPD to transform SMART targets

Most education provisions allocate staff meetings or teacher training days to deliver training to improve provision and practice for CYP with SEND.

To begin transforming how targets are created for CYP, you need to determine how SMART targets are made in your context.

Finding out activity
- Who currently writes CYP targets?
- How often are targets reviewed (not in policy but reality, as evidenced on the school monitoring systems)?

Once you have the information from the previous activity, you will know and understand your context's systems, processes and development needs. The following sections share approaches to leading CPD to transform target setting. You will need to adapt these based on your findings from the previous activity.

CPD session 1: setting the scene and making a start (15–20 minutes)

It is essential for anyone leading a CPD session for colleagues to ensure all those attending have a solid, basic understanding of the legal and regulatory requirements. Without this foundation, those attending the CPD session may be less clear on what you advocate and why, or they may feel less confident to change practice. The following outline is a suggested CPD activity you may wish to deliver with your colleagues to make a start on developing and improving SMART targets in your setting.

1a   Briefly summarise the purpose of the CPD session.
1b   Share Table 1.2 with your colleagues and ask them to raise any queries concerning the table content.
1c   Hand out a copy of Table 1.4 (which is photocopiable) and ask colleagues if the targets in Table 1.4 reflect the requirements of a SMART

Table 1.4 CPD session 1: are these targets SMART?

To act in an age-appropriate manner	To enter the classroom quickly and quietly	To always listen
To participate in class discussions	To show awareness of personal space	To realise you can change your behaviour
To sit still	To think before speaking	To be aware of the feelings of others
To behave nicely	To believe in yourself	To exercise greater self-control
To follow instructions in a prompt and sensible manner	To stay away from others who make you misbehave	To make eye contact when an adult talks to you
To pass all General Certificate of Secondary Education (GCSE) exams in the summer	To be able to accept praise	To complete all set tasks
To show sensitivity when dealing with peers	To always meet behaviour expectations	To take responsibility for own behaviour
To think about the consequences for your actions	To remember your behaviour negatively reflects on your family	To think about the impact of others when you do not listen
To get better at handwriting	To understand times tables	To use punctuation

target (specific, measurable, achievable, relevant and time-bound) as noted in Table 1.3.

Optional: You may wish to include some targets currently in use on SEN support plans in your setting.

1d Give feedback and reflect: ask participants their thoughts and reflections from the activity.

CPD session 2: Bloom's taxonomy

To promote reflective practice when setting out, writing and managing SMART targets for CYP, you are advised to introduce colleagues to Bloom's taxonomy of educational objectives (Table 2.1).

It is worthwhile to establish knowledge and understanding around Bloom's taxonomy and to use the following as an introduction or as a refresher or recap.

Bloom's taxonomy

The original taxonomy of educational objectives (Bloom, 1956) included six categories of cognitive processes ranging from simple to complex (knowledge, comprehension, application, analysis, synthesis and evaluation). Each level represents an essential skill for children to become critical thinkers (Murphy, 2007). Bloom believed that the taxonomy was a step process; to achieve the higher category, you must master the lower categories (Agarwal, 2019). In the revised version (Anderson et al., 2001), the taxonomy illustrates learning in verb tense (see Table 2.1), with higher-order categories, including apply, analyse, evaluate and create. It provides verbs associated with each level of learning. For example, understanding requires less knowledge than evaluating. Another example is that remembering a skill is not as difficult as applying it in different situations. This should be used as a guide when supporting and training staff in writing SMART targets where the outcome is observable.

In discussing Bloom's taxonomy, it may be helpful to ask colleagues for examples of how they use different cognitive processing levels in their

Table 1.5 Useful verbs: based on Bloom's taxonomy

	Cognitive process	SMART targets: common verbs
Lower-order thinking skills	Remembering	Cite, copy, describe, define, find, google, identify, illustrate, list, locate, memorise, match, name, outline, quote, recollect, recall, recognise, record, relate, remind, repeat, retrieve, state, tell and underline
	Understanding	Add, ask, annotate, answer, approximate, articulate, associate, categorise, compare, choose, cite, classify, contrast, describe, determine, differentiate, discriminate, discuss, explain, express, extract, generalise, identify, infer, interpret, locate, paraphrase, pick, report, restate, review, recognise, select, tag, tell, translate, tweet, relate, respond, restate, practise, simulate and summarise
	Applying	Act, apply, articulate, demonstrate, carry, change, choose, complete, cook, construct, crawl, cut, demonstrate, discover, display, dramatise, draw, dress, drink, drive, eat, employ, examine, execute, fasten, generalise, illustrate, implement, initiate, interpret, judge, loading, measure, operate, operationalise, paint, perform, practise, read, re-enact, relate, ride, schedule, show, sing, sketch, solve, stir, teach, throw, transfer, translate, travel, use, utilise, wait, walk and wash
Higher-order thinking skills	Analysing	Analyse, appraise, break down, calculate, categorise, compare, conclude, connect contrast, correlate, criticise, deduce, debate, detect, determine, develop, diagnose, diagram, differentiate, deduce, distinguish, divide, estimate, evaluate, examine, experiment, identify, illustrate, infer, inspect, investigate, interpret, link, measure, organise, predict, question, relate, solve, take apart and test
	Evaluating	Accept, appraise, argue, assess, capture, check, choose, compare, conclude, critique, defend, estimate, evaluate, express, judge, justify, measure, organise, predict, prioritise, select, rank, rate, recommend, revise, review, score, select, support, test, validate and value
	Creating	Adapt, animate, arrange, assemble, author, bake, blog, build, collect, compose, construct, craft, create, design, develop, devise, direct, display, exhibit, film, formulate,

(Continued)

21

Table 1.5 (Continued) Useful verbs: based on Bloom's taxonomy

Cognitive process	SMART targets: common verbs
	generate, illustrate, invent, make, manage, model, modify, negotiate, organise, photograph, plan, podcast, prepare, produce, propose, predict, programme, reconstruct, role play, sculpt, set up, simulate, sketch, solve, stick, storyboard, synthesise, systematise, wiki build and write

Adapted from Anderson et al. (2001) Bloom's taxonomy

everyday lives. This could help develop an appreciation that everyone applies different levels of thinking skills at various times of the day, including CYP.

CPD session 3: developing and understanding SMART targets

3a Prepare and provide colleagues with a range of targets gathered from current support plans within your setting that they are using or have used recently. Alternatively, you can use the following case study:

Case study: Jack

Jack has recently transitioned from primary school (in nurture provision) to mainstream secondary school. He arrived at the school without an SEN support plan, and the SENCO is currently applying for an EHC needs assessment. Jack has a diagnosis of autism and attention deficit hyperactivity disorder (ADHD). Jack responds well to routine; he is academically able but has difficulty dealing with unexpected changes. When anxious, he displays repetitive behaviours and can become disruptive in class if not supported. When interested in a lesson, he is hyper-focused; though if not, he cannot concentrate and will disrupt other children by repeatedly leaving his seat. Jack has

Table 1.6 Targets for Jack

The target	Specific	Measurable	Achievable	Relevant	Time-bound
To sit still	✓	✓	✗	✗	✗
To make eye contact when an adult talks to him	✓	✓	✗	✗	✗
To travel home from school on his own, once, by November	✓	✓	✓	✓	✓
To always meet behaviour expectations	✗	✓	✗	✗	✗
To be able to ride the bus to and from school on his own, by Christmas break	✓	✓	✓	✓	✓
Not to react when a routine changes	✗	✗	✗	✗	✗
To get better at expressing feelings of anxiety	✗	✗	✗	✗	✗
To deal with change	✗	✗	✗	✗	✗

expressed that he would like to travel to school independently, though he worries the bus will be late or miss the stop. His mother feels it is time for him to become more independent and less reliant on her for transport.

3b   Reflect on current SEN support plans (60 minutes).
- Ask colleagues to work together to reflect on and record the SMARTness of different targets on current SEN support plans that you gathered ready for the session (20 minutes).

If using the case study for Jack, add a range of targets you would like your colleagues to think about and discuss. It will be easy for them to decide if each target is specific, measurable and time-bound. However, to determine if it is achievable and relevant, they will need to think of a child they have experience of supporting.

- Reflect on how SMART the current SEN support and EHCP targets are, using SEN support plans and EHCPs that you have collected from within your setting (in line with Data Protection and Safeguarding requirements), and discuss/propose suggestions on how they could be improved. Encourage participants to put in bold the common verb for each target drawn from suggestions outlined in Bloom's taxonomy discussed earlier (20 minutes).

3c Build SMARTness (5 minutes).
   • Use and share the following example with colleagues.

SMART targets

Sarah, age 10, is on the SEN register for SEN support for social, emotional and mental health (SEMH). She has low self-confidence and anxiety due to multiple previous fixed-period and permanent exclusions. Sarah has a diagnosis of dyscalculia which affects her ability to estimate, organise and recall number bonds and times tables. Sarah has a reduced reading speed due to her dyslexia and her challenges with decoding and dropping a line when reading. This has affected both her comprehension and confidence. Her mother has explained that Sarah previously enjoyed reading but in recent months has become disinterested. Sarah has expressed to her teacher that she would like to read some of her friends' books (by Jacqueline Wilson) and not feel so behind in maths lessons. The following plan was devised in consultation with Sarah and her caregiver.

3d Ask colleagues to apply what they have learned by revisiting and reworking the targets outlined in the SEN support plans and EHCPs you gathered, making annotations of their ideas and thoughts and key aspects of the new proposed target. Here are example:
   1 Where the CYP's voice is included
   2 Where the caregiver's voice and knowledge are included
   3 Where there is evidence of partnership working

The participants will also need to consider how and when they could implement the new targets being proposed and any other professionals that need to input their voice into the support plan or EHCP to reflect the new proposed targets. It is important to ensure that during the discussion and remodelling, colleagues check if their new proposed target does meet the criteria of being SMART.

Table 1.7 Example SEN support plan for plenary activity

Target (specific)	Measurable	Achievable	Relevant	Time-bound
To choose from a selection of short decodable books to read for 5 minutes each day	Teacher observation	We have a wide selection of decodable books with a range of genres	Adult available to support and 'feeling good book' in use in class Mum is keen in reading the 'feeling good book' with Sarah at home	To read for 5 minutes each day
To select manipulatives to show pairs of numbers that total 20 by February half-term	Teacher observation	Sarah can add more confidently when she has the use of manipulatives	This target will support Sarah with her attainment in mathematics	To achieve by February 2022
To make a film with friends about the author Jacqueline Wilson to show in an assembly during Children's Book Week 2022	Teacher assessed through the planning and making of the film	Sarah has an interest in the author Jacqueline Wilson and has basic film-making skills	Sarah has an interest in the author Jacqueline Wilson and an aspiration to be a film director and podcaster	To have the film ready for May 3, 2022

Post-CPD activity: The annotated copies will provide evidence of the learning because of the CPD. Over time, it will be necessary to continue to monitor the effectiveness of SMART targets, set alongside how well they capture and reflect the views, wishes and feelings of CYP and their caregivers.

REFLECTIVE ACTIVITY

Earlier in the chapter, you were asked to find out about the systems and processes in your setting to create SMART targets. Reflect on your responses using a simple RAG rating system:

- **Red** – Significant action required
- Amber – Attention needed
- Green – The evidence suggests processes and systems are robust

Using Table 2.6 as an example, determine your action plan and next steps (for SEN support plans and a second table for the RAG rating systems and processes for EHCPs) (Table 1.8).

Table 1.8 Capturing and responding to the views, wishes and feelings to inform SEN support plans

Question	RAG rating	Concern	Plan of action
1. Who decides the CYP's targets (individual class teachers, support staff, subject leads, form tutors, pastoral lead, SENCO, CYP or caregivers)?		SENCO sets all targets in the school but does not always have a good knowledge or understanding of the child's needs or attainment	To propose a new system to the Senior Leadership Team (SLT) to transfer responsibility for SEN support plan writing to form tutors and pastoral leads by April 2023. To schedule further CPD to upskill staff in capturing views, wishes and feelings of CYP and their caregivers by January 2023
2. How and when are targets decided?		SEN support plans are reviewed termly as set out in the SEND code of practice (DfE and DoH, 2015); however, they are not co-produced with CYP or caregivers	See the plans of action for questions 1 and 3

Question	RAG rating	Concern	Plan of action
3. Where does the information come from to inform the plan?		Information to inform the plans comes from the SENCO's knowledge and understanding of the child and previous SEN support plans	To setup a new recording system in the school for form tutors and pastoral leads to record CYP and caregiver views, wishes and feelings To have SENCO and pastoral team write a good practice guide on capturing views, wishes and feelings of CYP and their caregivers, to disseminate and implement by April 2023
4. Are targets co-produced with the CYP, caregiver, teacher and other agencies?		If there are recommendations from external agencies, the SENCO includes these in current plans	See the plans of action for questions 1 and 3
5. How are CYP and caregivers involved in the process?		Currently, the SENCO sets the targets and does not have the capacity (due to full-time teaching) to include CYP or caregiver voice	See the plans of action for questions 1 and 3
6. Are the plans for the caregivers and children? If not, who are they for?		The plans are currently a tick-box exercise and are not consistently used by teachers and support staff.	To plan, deliver, evaluate and monitor the impact of termly CPD sessions to the whole staff on legal and regulatory duties for provision and practice of CYP with SEND by January 2023
7. Do the targets link to the child's SEN as identified on their SEN register?		As a SENCO, I audited the SEN register against targets and identified inconsistencies	To review all SEN support plans against the type of SEN on the SEN register by January 2023
9. How SMART do you think your targets are?		Currently, targets are not SMART across the school	To review on April 2023

Chapter summary

- Legal requirements underpin children's rights, as outlined in the CAFA (2014) and the UNCRC (UNICEF, 1989). This convention underpins the Equality Act (2010) and the CAFA (2014).
- Fundamental principles support the use of and need for SMART targets that meet the needs of CYP within education settings.
- SMART targets can be applied to any setting where children require additional support or assistance, whether medical, social or educational.

 ## Further reading and useful resources

Brokenbrow, L., Horridge, K. and Stair, H. (2016) *Disability matters in Britain 2016: Enablers and challenges to inclusion for disabled children, young people and their families.* London: Royal College of Paediatrics and Child Health.

Council for Disabled Children (2017) *Education, health and care plans: Examples of good practice.* London: Council for Disabled Children.

Council for Disabled Children (2021) *Education, health and care plans: Examples of good practice from year 9 and beyond.* London: Council for Disabled Children.

References

Agarwal, P.K. (2019) 'Retrieval practice and Bloom's taxonomy: Do students need fact knowledge before higher-order learning?', *Journal of Educational Psychology*, 111(2), pp. 189–209.

Anderson, L.W. et al. (2001) *A taxonomy for learning, teaching, and assessing: A revision of Bloom's taxonomy of educational objectives.* New York: Addison Wesley Longman.

Bloom, B.S. (1956) *Taxonomy of educational objectives; the classification of educational goals.* New York: Longmans, Green.

Buck, D. (2015) 'Reconstructing educational psychology reports: An historic opportunity to change educational psychologists' advice?', *Educational Psychology in Practice*, 31(3), pp. 221–234.

Children Act 1989. Available at: https://www.legislation.gov.uk/ukpga/1989/41/contents

Children and Families Act (CAFA) 2014. Available at: https://www.legislation.gov.uk/ukpga/2014/6/contents/enacted (Accessed: 25 November 2021).

Department for Children, Schools and Families (DCSF) (2009) *Lamb Inquiry: Special educational needs and parental confidence*. Nottingham: DCSF.

Department for Education (DfE) (1994) *The Special educational needs code of practice*. Nottingham: DfE.

Department for Education (DfE) (2014) *The Equality Act 2010 and schools: Departmental advice for school leaders, school staff, governing bodies and local authorities*. London: DfE.

Department for Education (DfE) and Department of Health (DoH) (2015) *Special educational needs and disability code of practice: 0 to 25 years: Statutory guidance for organisations which work with and support children and young people who have special educational needs or disabilities*. London: DfE.

Department for Education and Skills (DfES) (2001) *Special educational needs code of practice*. London: DfES.

Desforges, C. and Abouchaar, A. (2003) *The Impact of parental involvement, parental support and family education on pupil achievement and adjustment: A literature review*. London: Department for Education and Skills.

Doyle, W. (1986) 'Content representation in teachers' definitions of academic work', *Journal of Curriculum Studies*, 18(4), pp. 365–379. doi:10.1080/0022027860180402.

Driver Youth Trust (2015) *Joining the dots: Have the recent reforms worked for those with SEND?* London: Driver Youth Trust.

Emmer, E. and Stough, L. (2001) 'Classroom management: A critical part of educational psychology, with implications for teacher education', *Educational Psychologist*, 36(2), pp. 103–112.

Equality Act 2010, c. 15. Available at: http://www.legislation.gov.uk/ukpga/2010/15/contents (Accessed: 7 May 2020).

Gillett-Swan, J.K. (2013) *Time to tell: The complexity of wellbeing from the perspective of tweens*. PhD dissertation, Australian Catholic University.

Gillett-Swan, J.K. (2014) 'Investigating tween children's capacity to conceptualise the complex issue of wellbeing', *Global Studies of Childhood*, 4(2), pp. 64–78.

Goodall, J. and Vorhaus, J. (2011) *Review of best practice in parental engagement*. London: Department for Education.

Gross, J. (2000) 'Paper promises? Making the Code work for you', *Support for Learning*, 15(3), pp. 126–133. doi: 10.1111/1467-9604.00161.

House of Commons (2019) *Special educational needs and disabilities: First report of session 2019*. London: House of Commons.

House of Commons Education Committee (2018) *Forgotten children: Alternative provision and the scandal of ever-increasing exclusions: Fifth report of session 2017–2019*. London: House of Commons.

Hunter, J., Runswick-Cole, K., Goodley, D. and Lawthom, R. (2019) *Plans that work: Improving employment opportunities for young disabled people*. Available at: https://www.ippr.org/files/ 2019-04/ plans-that-work-april 19.pdf. (Accessed: 9 March 2022).

Independent Provider of Special Education Advice (IPSEA) (2021) *Asking for an EHC needs assessment*. Available at: https://www.ipsea.org.uk/ asking-for-an-ehc-needs-assessment (Accessed: 31 October 2021).

Martin-Denham, S. (2020a) *The enablers and barriers to mainstream schooling: The voices of children excluded from school, their caregivers, and professionals*. Sunderland: University of Sunderland.

Martin-Denham, S. (2020b) *The enablers and barriers to successful managed moves: The voice of children, caregivers, and professionals*. Sunderland: University of Sunderland.

Martin-Denham, S. (2020c) *A review of school exclusion on the mental health, wellbeing of children and young people in the City of Sunderland*. Sunderland: University of Sunderland.

Martin-Denham, S. (2020d) 'Riding the rollercoaster of school exclusion coupled with drug misuse: The lived experience of caregivers', *Emotional and Behavioural Difficulties*, 25(3–4), pp. 244–263.

Martin-Denham, S. (2021) 'The varying alternatives to school exclusion: Interviews with headteachers in England', *Emotional and Behavioural Difficulties*, pp. 1–19.

Martin-Denham, S. (2022) 'Autism and school exclusion: Caregiver's reflections', [Accepted: *Support for Learning*].

Martin-Denham, S. and Watts, S. (2019) *SENCO handbook: Leading provision and practice*. London: SAGE Publications, Ltd.

Merrick, R. (2020) 'Pupil participation in planning provision for special educational needs: Teacher perspectives', *Support for Learning*, 35(1), pp. 101–118.

Murphy, E.J. (2007) 'A Review of Bloom's Taxonomy and Kolb's theory of experiential Learning: Practical uses for prior learning assessment', *Journal of Continuing Higher Education*, 55(3), pp. 64–66.

Ofsted (1999) *The SEN Code of Practice: Three years on*. Nottingham: DfES.

Partridge, A. (2005) 'Children and young people's inclusion in decision-making', *Support for Learning*, 20(4), pp. 181–189. doi: 10.1111/j.0268-2141.2005.00386.x

Räty, L., Vehkakoski, T. and Pirttimaa, R. (2019) 'Documenting pedagogical support measures in Finnish IEPs for students with intellectual disability', *European Journal of Special Needs Education*, 34(1), pp. 35–49.

Sales, N. and Vincent, K. (2018) 'Strengths and limitations of the Education, Health and Care plan process from a range of professional and family perspectives', *British Journal of Special Education*, 45, pp. 61–80.

UNICEF (1989) *The United Nations Convention on the Rights of the Child*. London: UNICEF.

2 Creative approaches to capturing views, wishes and feelings of caregivers and children

Sarah Martin-Denham and Wendy Thorley

Settings will be at various stages in how well they listen to and respond to CYP and their caregivers. This chapter accepts and recognises that listening to CYP is a growing initiative that has led to research projects, such as Voice of the Pupil (Schools North East (NE)) and Pupil Voice Week (an initiative started by tootoot, involving over 600 schools from 27 September to 1 October 2021). Building on these projects, this chapter aims to specifically support listening to children's views, wishes and feelings in everyday provision and practice. The chapter contains case studies from individual children and their caregivers, and includes how their views shaped provision and practice.

School exclusions: child and caregiver voice

Research on factors leading to school exclusion has shown that involving children and caregivers improves CYP's outcomes (Martin-Denham, 2020a). Positive relationships and school-wide systems that support a person-centred ethos are fundamental to creating a sense of belonging (Martin-Denham, 2020a, 2020b, 2020c, 2020d). Both children's and their caregivers' voices are needed if meaningful participation is to be achieved. In the study involving 41 caregivers and 55 CYP from 5 to 16 years, it was evident that they could articulate and share insights into what support would have helped them participate and learn in school, as shown in Figures 2.1, 2.2, 2.3 and 2.4 (Martin-Denham, 2020a):

 DOI: 10.4324/9781003261506-3

'What could have helped you stay in mainstream school?'

'I could have been helped by going to nurture group.'

'To bring in teddies and fidget cubes.'

'Having time to talk room.'

'If I had some targets; I have targets now.'

Figure 2.1 The views of children in key stage 1 (p. 76)

'If someone had sat and explained the work, I would have done it. I would have understood it.'

'I wasn't going to run out of school; I just wanted to go on the track. I prefer to be outside. I like fresh air and doing outdoor stuff.'

'Definitely a quiet room. Not noisy and stressful. I would say put me in lessons where I know people. Where I get on with them, even just a few weeks to get settled in.'

Figure 2.2 The views of children in key stages 2 and 3 (p. 76)

'Talk to me and help with my work. They wouldn't help me. Then I would end up kicking off, distracting people because I had nothing to do' and 'give more support with work instead of removing from lessons.'

'It's good to not to be so harsh on every single thing you do. What difference does it make if your shirt is out or in? It's not going to affect how you learn.'

Figure 2.3 The views of children in key stage 4 (p. 77)

33

'He was just classed as the naughty boy. I don't think they understood his syndrome' and 'fidgeting as well... They try to get him to stand in a line. We know he's not going to stand still, so he gets told off and gets detention. But they know he can't do it, so why make him?

'Stick by the plans; they haven't got the staff or resources to do it; a lot of it is about resources, I think.' (EHCP)

'We were never given a copy of his support plan until they excluded him.'

'They needed to listen. They were very quick just to say he was naughty.'

Figure 2.4 The views of caregivers
(p. 78)

Sharing information with caregivers or involving caregivers earlier could have reduced the risk of school exclusion.

Recognising when children are trying to have their voice heard

When trying to retain control over busy classrooms, it is understandable that teachers and support staff may miss children's non-verbal signals indicating they are beginning to struggle emotionally within the setting. The need to listen to children and recognise how 'behaviour is communication' has been increasingly recognised and understood through the work evolving out of Adverse Childhood Experiences (ACEs) projects, particularly regarding neurological development functioning. Thorley and Townsend's (2017) 'What survival looks like in secondary school' highlighted how children's 'feel' informs behaviours that are seen. The guide includes 'what I look like', 'what I am aware of', 'how my body feels' and 'what's happening in my inner world' (pp. 8, 17–19). They proposed a range of actions for teachers and support staff to implement within the setting that could reduce stressors for CYP, which would de-escalate some of the difficulties they were exposed to. Although developed for children who had traumatic childhood experiences, such as Zak (living with domestic violence), they are suitable for many CYP, such as those who have been bullied. Here are examples:

- Don't stand over me if I am struggling with the task. Talk to the whole class and explain further so everyone hears and I am not singled out.
- Don't ask me questions in front of everyone by name. Ask if anyone knows the answer so I can join in when I feel it is safe.
- Accept that things you might think are just 'messing about' may make me feel like I am under attack by others.
- Let me choose where to sit so I can find somewhere that does not make me feel threatened. It might be at the back of the class so no one is behind me, or it might be at the front of the class nearer to you.
- Try not to get annoyed with me if I have forgotten where I was or what I was supposed to be doing; remind me alongside my friends gently.
- Don't tell everyone if my work is not good enough; let me know and give me a time when I can come to speak to you one-to-one without everyone else listening in. This includes CYP, their caregivers and other members of staff.
- Allow me to choose who I feel safe with to talk to; don't tell me I have to talk to a specific member of staff.
- Let me pick where to sit and which groups I work with.

Thorley and Townsend's (2017) suggestions reflect 'child voice' in that Thorley wrote the guide when he was 14, based on his own school experiences. Martin-Denham (2020a, 2020b, 2020c, 2020d) shared CYP's voices, highlighting that they understand their world and can articulate what support they need.

A working together plan is a useful way of capturing how the child feels and which behaviours they display in times of calm and distress. Including CYP's and caregivers' voices should underpin any working together plan developed in the setting. The purpose of the plan is to be proactive and allow those working with the CYP to recognise early indicators of anxiety so support can be promptly put into place. By creating a working together plan, the child may also identify their early indicators of distress, as highlighted by Thorley and Townsend (2017).

Working together plans

The Challenging Behaviour Foundation developed and devised positive behaviour support plans (BSP) to provide proactive strategies to ensure the CYP is provided with what they need (The Challenging Behaviour Foundation, 2021). For this chapter, the BSPs have been renamed to working together plans to recognise that behaviour is communication. Working together plans move the focus from behaviour to co-production of a range of strategies for early intervention, specifically around individual needs, including the views and suggestions of CYP and their caregivers. In working together plans, the colours green, amber, red and blue relate to different stages of dysregulation, as follows:

> Green: calm and relaxed
> Amber: anxious, aroused and distressed
> Red: challenging behaviour incident (crisis)
> Blue: calming down – but still need to be careful
> > (The Challenging Behaviour Foundation, 2021, p. 6)

Case study 1: Zak

Zak, aged 11, lived with his mother, father and three siblings. His father was drug and alcohol dependent, and had become increasingly violent and aggressive in recent months. On Christmas Eve, his father went to the pub with his friends and came home at 11 pm to continue drinking. At 3 am, Zak's mother called the police as she was fearful that her partner would become violent once his friends left. The police arrived and told the father to find somewhere else to stay for the next 48 hours, he refused, and the police left the family home. Later, the father became aggressive towards the mother and threw her against the wall. Zak was standing on the landing and witnessed the attack. The father was taken into custody, and the mother remained at home with the children.

After the school holidays, Zak's mum informed the school of the events over Christmas. Zak had become increasingly distressed at home, fighting with his siblings and hitting his mother. The teachers had noticed significant changes in his behaviour at school. For example, Zak would hurt particular children during contact sports in PE or crowded corridors. He would scratch his face, pull his hair and withdraw from group work in class. With the school counsellor, Zak made LEGO models (Figures 2.5 and 2.6). The conversation is captured in the quotes embedded in the photos.

Figure 2.5 LEGO models made by Zak

Figure 2.6 LEGO models made by Zak

Zak's homelife was unpredictable and unstable over the Christmas period. As adults, we can often rationalise actions taken to provide a stable environment for children. However, the reasoning behind decisions made and any actions following these decisions are not always easily understood by the children impacted most. Involving Zak and his mother in the co-production of a working together plan (Table 2.1) gave Zak a voice and reflects the suggestions made by Thorley and Townsend (2017) for CYP who have experienced traumatic events in their lives. By sharing his views, wishes

Table 2.1 Zak's working together plan

Working together plan: Zak

What I find difficult

1 Separating from the teacher at the end of the school day
2 Playing contact sports and losing games
3 Being in crowds
4 Having physical contact

Green	
Support strategies	**What Zak will do and say when he is calm and happy**
Tell me in advance if we are going to be doing rugby or football	• I will talk to my friends
	• I will answer questions
Don't put me on the opposite team to Danny or Tom	• I will smile sometimes
	• I will look at the teachers
Don't keep asking me if I am okay	
Let me leave the classroom 2 minutes early so I am not in a crowded corridor	

Amber	
Support strategies	**What Zak will do, say and look like showing he is *becoming* anxious and agitated**
Sit me with my best friend, Mabel	• I will talk to friends
Ask me to do a task that involves leaving the classroom or PE session	• I won't speak to men teachers
	• I won't answer questions in class
Allow me to walk off the pitch to go and see Ms Joe (pastoral office)	• I will ask to leave the class
	• I will get frustrated in PE and might walk off the pitch
Let the teachers know I might not always be able to talk to them	• I won't smile much
	• I will fidget in my seat
	• I will tap my pen
	• I will drop equipment on the floor

Red	
Support strategies	**What Zak will do when he is in crisis**
Stay calm and say you will help me	• I will stare
Give me space and allow me to be left alone	• I won't look at you
Get Ms Joe from the pastoral office if I do not regulate with space	• I might scratch my face or pull my hair
	• I might ask for space
Don't let me leave the classroom without supervision if it is a transition time for the school	• I might hit or try to fight other children
	• I will not be able to listen to men teachers
	• I won't be able to control my reactions if someone touches me

(Continued)

Table 2.1 (Continued) Zak's working together plan

Blue	
Support strategies	**What Zak does, says and looks like to tell us he is calming down**
'Help me quickly return to green (usually in a few minutes)' Ask me how you can help me; just knowing you care will help me regulate Check the other children aren't staring at me, as this can make the situation reoccur	• I will begin to look at you • I might ask you a random question; I do this to check you are okay with me • I will stop scratching my face or pulling my hair

Adapted from The Challenging Behaviour Foundation (2021)

and feelings, Zak was empowered to recognise when he struggled to cope. The development of the working together plan brought shared ideas and support to be provided by the school, social worker, other professionals and family members.

Case study 2: Filipa

Filipa, 6, was diagnosed with high-functioning autism when she was 5. She attended a mainstream primary school and was exceeding the expected level in the core subjects of the national curriculum (DfE, 2014). However, Filipa struggled with Personal, Social, Health and Economic (PSHE) education at school – to develop positive relationships with other children and adults (DfE, 2019). During the COVID-19 pandemic, there had been six different supply teachers due to the long-term illness of the permanent teacher.

Filipa found it hard to socialise with the other children. She often worked independently and could not work as part of a group. She would get very anxious during playtime when the children were outside of the classroom setting, often struggling to regulate or control her emotions. She expressed her dysregulation by biting other children and adults to communicate a need for personal space (usually when a child or adult was too close). Filipa would sit alone in the classroom and outdoors, and watch but

Figure 2.7 Filipa's drawing

not engage with other children who approached her. She had a particular interest in watermelons and liked incorporating them into her drawings. In preparation for her EHCP annual review, her teacher asked her to draw what she would like to be when she grows up (Figure 2.7). When they talked about the drawing, she told the teacher she wanted to be a fashion designer.

It was evident that Filipa preferred to communicate through her drawing and artistic expression. To ensure Filipa had a voice, her working together plan included opportunities to express her feelings and thoughts, as shown in Table 2.2.

Table 2.2 Filipa's working together plan

Working together plan: Filipa
What I find difficult
- Not having my teacher at school
- Not knowing what is happening next
- Experiencing sudden changes in routine

Green

Support strategies	What Filipa will do and say when she is calm and happy
Provide a daily visual timetable showing the daily routine Provide a weekly timetable showing which teachers are covering the class (with a surprise symbol) if the teacher is not yet in place Help Filipa establish connections with other children by providing 10 minutes a day of small group support, such as the following: • Making puppets for role play • Sharing stories • Completing a drawing for a friend • Writing a note for a friend • Playing alongside a friend	• I will be doing my schoolwork • I will sit near to other children in the class and talk to them • I will look happy • I will join in with other children

Amber

Support strategies	What Filipa will do, say and look like showing she is *becoming* anxious and agitated
Support Filipa in expressing her emotions: 'can I help you?' and 'Filipa, you can tell me, are you okay?' Ask Filipa if she would like to draw a picture • I will	• I will stop talking to the other children in my class • I will ask to draw a picture • I will bite my lip • I will turn my head away when someone talks to me • I will start to cry Provide something Filipa can safely bite on – a carrot stick or piece of watermelon

Red

Support strategies	What Filipa will do when she is in crisis
Remain calm and say, 'Filipa, no biting' and 'Filipa, biting hurts'	• I will try to bite other children and adults • I will cry (following a bite)

Start drawing watermelons and other fruits; in time, Filipa will join in

Guide Filipa towards the sensory room

Blue	
Support strategies	**What Filipa does, says and looks like to tell us she is calming down**
Ask Filipa if she would like to take part in an art-based activity (Play-Doh, sand art or drawing)	• I will talk to you • I will start drawing • I will say sorry
Reshare the daily visual timetable and talk about what is happening next	
Talk about what happened when Filipa regulates (green) – 'Filipa, why did you bite?' –and support the repairing of the relationship	

Adapted from The Challenging Behaviour Foundation (2021)

Allowing Filipa to express herself through her drawings means she can focus on a single activity of her choosing. When this takes place outside of the demands of the classroom setting, she can feel safe and supported.

Case study 3: Rey

Rey, aged 16, attended a further education (FE) college. Rey was diagnosed with congenital cataracts when he was 9 and, despite surgery, continued to have poor vision due to bilateral cataracts. His condition resulted in cloudy/blurry vision and difficulty seeing in poorly lit spaces. Rey's tutor had noticed he was becoming increasingly agitated during transitions in the college day. The behaviours Rey displayed were fist-clenching, head-banging and vocalisations (shouting and screaming). His tutor was keen to discover the underlying reasons for the behaviours using Rey's interest in digital technologies. Rey asked his tutor if he could use PowerPoint to show how he felt about walking through the corridors between his classes (Figure 2.8). The slide portrayed the vast amount of sensory information Rey was subjected to. Rey articulated that his sensory overload was due to crowded corridors and transition alarms. Congested corridors increased the

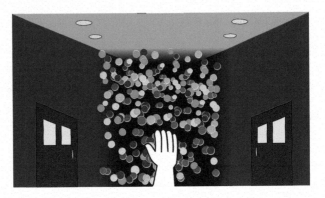

Figure 2.8 Rey's PowerPoint slide

Figure 2.9 Rey's guitar

noise levels from peers, and staff made it difficult for Rey to move around without bumping into people or displays. Rey has ear defenders but sometimes forgets to wear them.

Due to his sensory impairment, Rey told his tutor, 'I like doing activities where I can touch and hear things. Sometimes having a lot of people around me can be intense as well. That's why my favourite activity is playing my guitar'. Rey took photographs of his guitar (Figure 2.9) and favourite plectrum (Figure 2.10) to show to Dave. Rey likes the cool bright colours, making it harder for him to lose his plectrum.

Rey also told his tutor that he felt calmer when outdoors, with a lot more space than he had in the busy corridors. Rey felt that if he could leave sessions a little earlier, he would avoid the busiest times in the corridors. Leaving a few minutes earlier allowed Rey to go outside and reduce the level of sensory load. Rey produced an avatar (Figure 2.11) to help explain the difference it could make to him so that his tutor could see the difference between being in the corridors (his PowerPoint) and being outdoors (his avatar).

Figure 2.10 Rey's plectrum

Figure 2.11 Rey's avatar

Rey's working together plan was developed using the images he produced and listening to what he said helped him and what worked for him specifically (Table 2.3):

Table 2.3 Rey's working together plan

Working together plan: Rey
What I find difficult
- Being in noisy corridors and classrooms
- Being in dark places
- Moving between lessons

Green	
Support strategies	**What Rey will do and say when he is calm and happy**
Check Rey has his ear defenders during noisy classroom activities and for transition times	• I will take part in classroom activities and will tell you I am fine
Allow Rey to leave the classroom a few minutes before the other CYP to avoid corridor traffic	• I will arrive at lessons on time, take off my blazer and interact with friends
	• I will initiate a conversation with adults

Amber	
Support strategies	**What Rey will do, say and look like showing he is *becoming* anxious and agitated**
Stay calm, get down to Rey's level and ask him to put on his ear defenders	• I will clench my fists
Seek the pastoral team to take Rey for a walk outside	• I will stop smiling and might clench my fists
Allow Rey to leave the classroom a few minutes before the other CYP to avoid corridor traffic and ensure classroom noise levels are minimised	• I might start to randomly shout
Seek the pastoral team to take Rey to play his guitar	• I will wander around the classroom and won't want to be in my seat

Red	
Support strategies	**What Rey will do when he is in crisis**
Appear calm and talk in a quiet, reassuring voice; seek support from the pastoral team	• I will bang my head on the desk or wall
Place your hand gently on his shoulder	• I might hit my head with my fist
Don't shout or raise your voice, as this will escalate his self-harm	• I won't respond to your requests
	• I will cover my ears and shout

Blue	
Support strategies	What Rey does, says and looks like to tell us he is calming down
Help Rey quickly return to green (usually in a few minutes)	• I will stop headbanging and/or screaming
	• I will play my guitar
Ask Rey how you can help and don't demand he does his work	• I might still clench my fists, but this should stop in time
Allow Rey to play the guitar	• I will ask for lots of help with my work

Case study 4: Aya

Aya was diagnosed with dyslexia and dyscalculia when she was 11 years old and was added to the SEN register for her cognition and learning difficulties. Her mother arranged a meeting with the SENCO in the secondary school to discuss her support needs and to agree on the reasonable adjustments needed to prevent disadvantage:

• Use a blue overlay
• Use a light-blue background to support reading of the text
• Use no highlighted text or underline
• Use the Calibri font

During the meeting, Aya shared her views and thoughts on what would help her learn at school. Together, they created an SEN support plan (Table 2.4).

When she was 12 years old, Aya became increasingly frustrated by teachers not following her SEN support plan. The plan would only be effective if it was consistently implemented by all those who taught her. Aya became increasingly anxious and withdrew from talking to teachers, regardless of context (lessons, corridors and one-to-one). 'I always get the lowest score. I can't keep up. It's too fast. I want to be as good as the others, but I can't'.

One evening, after school, Aya shared a drawing with her mother to show her feelings (Figure 2.12). The picture was shared with the SENCO, and the following changes were made:

• All conversations with Aya would not take place in an office
• A 'pass' was issued so Aya could leave the classroom for a regulation break
• One-to-one support emotional support was provided by Ms Clegsworth

Table 2.4 Aya's SEN support plan

Things I find difficult (child-led)	My targets (child-, SENCO/ teacher- and parent-led)	What I can do (child-led)	Who's going to help me and when? (adult-led)	How did I get on? (child-led)
Remembering to pack my bag for my lessons and to bring my homework to school	To identify what I need for school before I leave the house To check I have everything I need	I will check my planner, timetable and the VLE every evening to know I have everything I need for the next day (PE kit, equipment, baking ingredients and homework)	I will set a reminder on my phone at 6 pm to get my backpack ready My form tutor will check I have remembered what I need at 9 am and if not, ring home	I find my alarms help the most; my form tutor sometimes forgets to check I have everything, and I am too shy to ask
Finding my way to lessons; I get easily lost	To arrive at all my lessons on time	I will make a colour-coded timetable in my intervention time to help me recognise where I need to be I will ask adults if I get lost	I will check my timetable with my mum in the morning to plan where I need to go when I get to school I will ask an adult to help me if I get lost in the school day	I find checking the timetable in the morning has helped; I got to most of my lessons on time
Reading my handwriting for revision	To read and summarise the notes I take in class	I need to type my notes rather than handwrite them, as I cannot read my writing and I struggle with spelling	Mum will provide me with a laptop for school use, and teachers will be informed that I am always to use this	I can read my notes from class, and I like that I can change the background colour easily

Figure 2.12 Aya's views, age 12

Case study 5: Will

Will is 3 years old and attends nursery in a mainstream primary setting. He was very settled until his father died unexpectedly when another car drove into him on his way home from work. Will's father was a keen amateur rally driver and outdoor activity parent, often walking, swimming, canoeing, dinghy sailing and rally driving with Will. Will told everyone his father was his hero.

Will returned to nursery but withdrew from joining in as much as he used to. Before the accident, Will was very much part of a group; since the accident, he answered questions using one-word yes or no answers and moved slightly outside of the group when playing. Will sat alone and drew a picture of learning to fly a kite with his father (Figure 2.13). Staff noticed he was eating less and some days would not eat his lunch. The nursery understood this was a difficult time for Will and his family, and developed

49

Figure 2.13 and *Figure 2.14* Will's drawings

a working together plan (Table 2.5) to help him adjust to his new home circumstances.

The nursery provided Will with a key worker, Katy, who had been working with Will since his return. In time, he told Katy he would like to be a rally driver when he is bigger (Figure 2.14). Will told Katy that 'you can't talk about 'daddy' because it makes everybody sad. I am sad'. He carried a small toy his father gave him zipped in his trouser or jacket pocket.

Table 2.5 Will's working together plan

Working together plan: Will	
Green	
Support strategies	**What Will will do and say when he is calm**
Let Will lead the discussion and support him if he wishes to talk about his father Repeat information given to Will by his family about death and his father as often as needed Ask Will if he would like Katy to look after his toy so it does not get lost Have all staff be aware of upcoming key dates or events, such as Father's Day and sports day as well as early years curriculum work focused around family	• I will take part in classroom activities • I will take off my coat when I arrive at nursery • I will talk to Katy or another child • I will give Katy my toy
Amber	
Support strategies	**What Will will do, say and look like when he is *becoming* anxious and agitated**
Stay calm, get down to Will's level and ask him if he would like to go and be with Katy Use visual aids to ask Will how he is feeling (emojis) Allow Will time to be by himself in the nursery if he prefers this; suggest the book corner where he can sit out Let Will sit with adult members of staff as an observer only if he chooses until he feels comfortable joining in	• I will clench my fists • I will stop smiling and might clench my fists • I might begin to cry • I will wander around the nursery and won't want to play or join other children

(Continued)

51

Table 2.5 (Continued) Will's working together plan

Red	
Support strategies	**What Will will do when he is in crisis**
Appear calm and talk in a quiet, reassuring voice until Katy can join Will; Katy will ask Will to go with her outside of the main activities Place your hand gently on his shoulder to help reassure Will Give to Will his comfort toy as soon as possible if the staff have it	• I will move away and go somewhere to be alone • I might cry or throw toys in the nursery • I won't respond to your requests
Blue	
Support strategies	**What Will does, says and looks like to tell us he is calming down**
Help Will return to green (usually in a few minutes) Allow Will to play with his comfort toy Allow Will to ask tricky questions about death, his father and what happens, and answer honestly using the same information his family provide for him Reassure Will – understand Will is confused and frightened about other people dying as well	• I will stop crying • I will play with my comfort toy from my dad quietly • I might still want to sit outside of the other children and main activities • I will tell you how I feel using the visual aid • I will answer your questions

Adapted from The Challenging Behaviour Foundation (2021)

Case study 6: Rosa

Rosa is 13 years old and currently living with her 7th foster family, having moved placement 4 months ago. Rosa moved into emergency foster care when she was 4, but due to several reasons outside of her control, she has required multiple foster care placements, having moved 3 times in the past 18 months. Social workers are hopeful this will be Rosa's final move, as the sense of insecurity increases with each move.

Following her emergency foster care placement, Rosa moved into two further foster homes then a longer-term placement that lasted five years.

Figure 2.15 Happy Rosa

During her time at this more extended placement, Rosa was happy and developing well, feeling very much part of the family, as shown in her drawing from that time (Figures 2.15 and 2.16).

Due to an unexpected change in the foster family circumstances, Rosa couldn't continue to live with the family. The family were as upset about the move as Rosa was. Rosa voiced how she felt in her drawing (Figure 2.16).

For some CYP, repeated traumatic periods in their lives can result in a submit behaviour, rather than fight, flight or freeze (discussed in Chapter 3).

Figure 2.16 How I feel about leaving my family

Thorley and Townsend (2017) suggested behaviour displayed by CYP during submit includes the following:

- Never questioning or asking questions, never drawing unnecessary attention
- Answering yes or no – doing just enough to get it done but not going further
- Being quiet and passive

Social workers discussed their concerns about Rosa's emotional health and wellbeing. Rosa was compliant in school; she followed the rules, sat quietly in class and completed the work. Her tutor agreed with the social worker that Rosa was compliant and appeared to complete all work as directed but only what was asked for specifically. The teacher confirmed Rosa did follow all rules but was not really engaged with others. Rosa's sense of insecurity had led to Rosa not engaging with her current foster carers. She preferred to sit in her room alone and only replied with yes-no answers during meal-times. Rosa spent her time alone outside of the classroom if she was able. She would sit alongside peers but wouldn't join in any conversations inside or outside the classroom.

Pip Wilson, a behavioural psychologist, developed the Blob Tree in the 1980s to help children communicate their feelings. The Blob Tree continues to be used with CYP and adults, and provides a visual resource to encourage them to share their thoughts (Wilson and Long, 2008, 2018). Rosa's social worker worked with Rosa using an iPad to draw and the Blob Tree principles. She explained to Rosa what a Blob Tree was and asked Rosa to place herself on the tree. The social worker gave Rosa three scenarios: her classroom, a social area in school and her foster family home. Using the iPad, Rosa placed herself very much on the outside looking in for all the drawings she made (Figure 2.17). Rosas's sense of not fitting in was also depicted in the colours she used.

Figure 2.17 Rosa's drawing of where she felt comfortable in school social areas

55

The social worker and her tutor explained the Circle of Control principle to Rosa. The Circle of Control was developed by Steve Covey (1989) in his book, *The 7 Habits of Highly Effective People*. The approach has been adapted across a range of settings for CYP and adults. The social worker talked to Rosa about her placement moves and where she was now with her new foster family, to help her identify things she could control in her life. It was felt that this would help Rosa identify where she could influence her life choices and identify a circle of support she could access. Rosa's tutor worked with the pastoral team to identify support available while she was in school. Rosa's social worker worked with the foster carers to identify support outside of school. The social worker and the foster carers also identified a range of activities to help Rosa build her self-confidence and self-esteem.

In school, her tutor, social worker, foster carers and pastoral staff worked with Rosa to develop her working together plan (Table 2.6), developing on her circle of control.

Table 2.6 Rosa's working together plan

Working together plan: Rosa
What I find difficult
• Believing I am not going to have to move again
• Making friends
• Feeling like I belong
• Being put in the spotlight

Green	
Support strategies	**What Rosa will do and say when she is calm and happy**
Tell me in advance of any changes to the timetable	• I will join classroom discussion as much as I feel comfortable
Don't have my social worker visit me in school	• I will answer questions
Don't keep asking me if I am okay	• I will smile sometimes
Don't tell me who I have to talk to about how I feel or personal things	• I will look at the teachers
Appreciate that staying on my own or in my room lets me be by myself somewhere safe	• I will sit with other children during break periods as much as I feel comfortable

Appreciate that I will say whatever I think you want me to say

Plan small group tasks that I can contribute to but let me choose my group so I am not overwhelmed by powerful personalities

Understand I cannot cope being the centre of attention or the focus person – let me blend in and talk when I am ready

Be aware that I am an easy target and can be coerced easily to keep the peace

Amber

Support strategies	What Rosa will do, say and look like showing she is *becoming* anxious and agitated
Give me a place to be myself – look for what I might be good at but don't focus on me or single me out for this Ask me to do a task that involves leaving the immediate area Allow me to find the pastoral team to sit with Let the teachers know I might not always be able to join in discussions	• I will stop talking to anyone unless asked a direct question • I will only answer with yes, no, don't know or don't mind • I will look away or down at my table in class • I will ask to leave the class • I won't smile • I will look like I am doing class work but won't do any more than I have to • I will remove myself to be by myself completely

Red

Support strategies	What Rosa will do when she is in crisis
Stay calm and say you will help me Understand that I need to talk to someone I feel safe with, not just anyone Listen to me and hear me when I talk Don't let me leave the classroom without letting the pastoral team know I am going there Recognise I am hurting inside and might need help	• I will stare out of a window or at the floor • I won't look at you or anyone else directly • I may cry but without making any sound • I will look sad • I might not answer any questions you ask me and shrug instead • I might look like I am ignoring you or other children if spoken to • I will try to make myself invisible so I am not noticed • I might try to remove myself when you are distracted or talking to others

(Continued)

Table 2.6 (Continued) Rosa's working together plan

Blue	
Support strategies	**What Rosa does, says and looks like to tell us she is calming down**
Help me quickly return to green (usually in a few minutes) Ask me if you can help me Be present near me so I know you are there when I am ready Check the other children aren't staring at me, as this can make the situation reoccur; distract them if necessary so I am not the focus of attention	• I will begin to look at you • I might move closer inside the area where you are or closer to you • I will start to answer you when you speak to me • I will move closer to other children • My physical body will look more relaxed and less tense • I will begin to complete work you have asked me to do

Adapted from The Challenging Behaviour Foundation (2021)

Chapter summary

- Most schools will have CYP who, at some time, have experienced difficult periods in their lives.
- Support for children through emotionally traumatic and challenging times is essential to supporting their learning overall.
- Behaviour as language should be listened to, as it is a key basis for developing a more supportive environment in which CYP can survive and thrive, be this inside or outside of the educational setting.
- CYP thoughts, feelings and desires can be generated through a range of approaches.
- Avatars and iPad drawings are familiar to CYP and provide ways in which they can express themselves.

Useful resources

Bereavement

Child Bereavement UK: Provides support to families and professionals when a child dies or when a child is bereaved of someone important in their life. Website: www.childbereavementuk.org.

Childhood Bereavement Network (CBN): A hub for those working with bereaved children, young people and their families across the UK. Website: www.childhoodbereavementnetwork.org.uk/home.aspx.

Child Death Helpline: A telephone helpline for anyone affected by the death of a child, from pre-birth to the death of an adult child, however long ago and whatever the circumstances. Website: http://childdeathhelpline.org.uk.

Winston's Wish: Supports bereaved children up to the age of 18 through a whole range of activities, including a helpline, group work, residential events and resources. Website: www.winstonswish.org.

Trauma and loss

Beacon House (www.beaconhouse.org.uk): An online website with free resources on supporting children who have experienced trauma and loss.

Center for the Developing Child at Harvard University (https://developingchild.harvard.edu/resources): This site has extensive resources, including short videos that clearly show the impact on the developing brain. The director, Jack P. Shonkoff, MD, is highly regarded in this area and has developed an understanding of the difference between 'stress' and 'toxic stress'.

Child Trauma Academy (http://childtrauma.org/cta-library): This site provides a library of videos and reading developed by Dr Bruce Perry – internationally respected for his work in this area; their videos within the seven-slide series are very short but very informative resources.

Inner World Work (www.innerworldwork.co.uk): An online support and resource centre for caregivers who are supporting traumatised children; it has free whole-school and classroom resources to support professionals.

Vision

Guide Dogs: Children and young people's service (formerly Blind Children UK) offer a range of services and activities for CYP and provide advice for parents and teachers.

Look UK: An organisation that helps support families with children aged between 0 and 16 with vision problems. They have family support officers and help support families at home and in school.

Royal Society for Blind Children: Provides a range of services in London and across England and Wales for blind and partially sighted CYP, their families and the professionals who work alongside them.

VICTA: Supports CYP who are blind or partially sighted and their families across the UK.

Voice

Blob Shop (2021) *What are the Blobs? A feelosophy*. Available at: https://www.blobtree.com/pages/frontpage (Accessed: 6 December 2021).

The Challenging Behaviour Foundation (2021) *'Stop, look and listen to me': Engaging children and young people with severe learning difficulties*. Available at: https://www.challengingbehaviour.org.uk/wp-content/uploads/2021/04/Stop-Look-and-Listen-to-me.pdf (Accessed: 6 December 2021).

Wilson, P. and Long, I. (2008) *The book of blob feelings*. 1st edn. London: Routledge.

Wilson, P. and Long, I. (2018) *The big book of blobs*. London: Routledge.

Circle of control

Newton, C. (2021) *Circles of control.* Available at: https://www.clairenewton.co.za/my-articles/circles-of-control.html (Accessed: 5 December 2021).
Teachers Pay Teachers (2021) *Circle of control resources.* Available at: https://www.teacherspayteachers.com/Browse/Search:circle%20control/Price-Range/Free/Type-of-Resource/Activities (Accessed: 5 December 2021).

References

Covey, S.R. (1989) *The 7 habits of highly effective people: Restoring the character ethic.* Rev. ed. New York: Free Press.
Department for Education (DfE) (2014) *The national curriculum in England: Framework document.* London: DfE.
DfE (2019) *Relationships education, relationships and sex education (RSE) and Health Education Statutory guidance for governing bodies, proprietors, head teachers, principals, senior leadership teams, teachers.* London: DfE.
Martin-Denham, S. (2020a) *The enablers and barriers to mainstream schooling: The voices of children excluded from school, their caregivers, and professionals.* Sunderland: University of Sunderland.
Martin-Denham, S. (2020b) *The enablers and barriers to successful managed moves: The voice of children, caregivers, and professionals.* Sunderland: University of Sunderland.
Martin-Denham, S. (2020c) *A review of school exclusion on the mental health, wellbeing of children and young people in the City of Sunderland.* Sunderland: University of Sunderland.
Martin-Denham, S. (2020d) 'Riding the rollercoaster of school exclusion coupled with drug misuse: The lived experience of caregivers', *Emotional and Behavioural Difficulties,* 25(3–4), pp. 244–263.

The Challenging Behaviour Foundation (2021) *Resource – Positive behaviour support planning: Part 3.* Available at: https://www.challengingbehaviour.org.uk/understanding-challenging-behaviour/what-is-challenging-behaviour/resource-positive-behaviour-support-planning-part-3/ (Accessed: 5 December 2021).
Thorley, M. and Townsend, H. (2017) *What survival looks like in secondary school.* Inner World Work. Available at: http://www.innerworldwork.co.uk/wp-content/uploads/2017/04/Survival-In-Secondary-School.pdf

A virtual school head perspective

Jane Pickthall

In this chapter, a virtual school head (VSH) explains the importance of address-ing the particular needs of CYP that have, or have had in the past, children's services involvement, including those classed as children in need (CiN) and children in care (CiC). The chapter will explore some of the factors that most impact the educational outcomes of those who have experienced ACEs, such as abuse or neglect. In addition, there will be an exploration of how EHCPs, SEN support plans and Personal Education Plans (PEPs) (CiC only) can become a key driver for improvements in CYP's outcomes if the targets are clearly focused on their needs. Creating a safe environment with trusted adults is the foundation for enabling CYP to contribute authentically to their PEPs as they feel more able to speak out about how best they can be supported.

Why is this chapter important?

It is estimated that around one in seven CYP have either historic or current involvement with children's services in schools across England. Of these, almost half (48.1%) have identified special educational needs (SEN) compared with the general school population rate of 15.3% (DfE, 2021a). The attainment gap between CiN (this definition includes CiN, CPP (Child Protection Plan) and CiC) and the rest of the school pop-ulation remains high. The latest key stage 4 attainment data showing that the average Attainment 8 score for CiN was only 21.1 compared to 50.2 for non-CiN pupils in 2019/20 (when GCSEs were cancelled due to COVID-19) and, previously, 18.8 compared to 46.7 in 2018/19.

Attendance, school exclusions, school stability and the numbers remaining in mainstream at the end of key stage 4 are all significantly worse for CiN and contribute to poor educational outcomes. A child does not choose the family they are born into, and this group of our

DOI: 10.4324/9781003261506-4

most disadvantaged CYP need all the support they can get to address the impact of what they have experienced in their lives. We all have a part to play in creating more positive futures for those who have had the hardest starts in life, and this chapter aims to support professionals to identify how best to meet CYP needs in education.

Who is this chapter for?

There are so many people involved in the lives of children with a social worker, and each one has a part to play in supporting children in achieving educational success. In schools, this includes the Senior Leadership Team, SENCO, designated safeguarding lead, designated teacher for looked after children (LAC), pastoral leads, class teachers, support staff and lunchtime staff – anyone who encounters a CYP. Then there is the child's social worker, independent reviewing officer, foster carer or residential childcare officer. The Virtual School Team also has a role to play, whether in the form of direct support or through coordinating PEPs. Birth parents, adoptive parents and guardians may also find this chapter useful, especially if their child has additional needs and they are seeking further support through an SEN support plan or an EHCP. This chapter is, therefore, aimed at everyone working to support a child with social care experience.

In this chapter, *CiN* and *CiC* will be used unless referring to a specific group defined by the DfE, such as previously looked after. For many years, the term *LAC* has been used, but the abbreviation *LAC* is not liked by CYP who are in the care system as it has negative connotations with 'lacking'. For this reason, the phrase used in this chapter is 'children in care' (CiC).

What is a virtual school head?

The role of a virtual school head (VSH) came into existence in 2014 to strengthen and build upon the work of LA in the Looked After Children Education Services (LACES). The role became one of only six that are statutory for a LA to have in place the CAFA (2014). Until 2017, the VSH was only statutorily responsible for the educational outcomes of CiC, and although this is the group whose outcomes the LA are held to account over, the role now includes providing advice and information for previously LAC

Figure 3.1 Two heads are better than one

and having a broader, systemic role for CYP who have never had a social worker (DfE, 2018a, 2021b). The disadvantages faced by those that have experienced ACEs can be reduced considerably if staff receive high-quality and relevant training, and the right support is provided in a timely way.

The VSH role is very much about partnership working. The role is at a senior level in the LA, and many VSHs have had leadership experience in schools prior to taking on the role. A VSH is there to provide a combination of challenge and support to make sure the needs of CYP with experience of children's social care involvement are recognised and understood across the wider system, and that professionals work together to create the best environment for success. Figure 3.1 illustrates the additionality of a virtual school head.

Factors that impact most on educational outcomes

Much of the focus of the VSH is identifying factors that have the greatest impact on improving educational outcomes and seeking to improve the system around the CYP to better meet their needs. The Rees Centre, Oxford University, were one of the first academic institutions to draw attention to these factors through two seminal research projects (Sebba et al., 2015; Berridge et al., 2020). They brought together children's social care data (SSDA903 collection – information about children who are looked after) and education data (National Pupil Database) to identify what makes the greatest difference to the key stage 4 outcomes of young people that had experienced support from a social worker. We appear to have little or no control over some of these factors, but others can be influenced by school, children's social care and virtual schools. Between us, we can make a real difference.

Please note that these factors, which have the greatest impact on educational outcomes, have been identified through statistical modelling, and there are many children who buck the trends, through the right support at the right time and their own determination and hard work. The factors we are focusing on in this chapter are to make us more mindful about where we need to focus our attention. With a rethink, some reflection time and some changes in practice, these factors need not be a barrier to success.

Some of the factors shared in Table 3.1 are specifically for CiC, as their circumstances are more complex and care decisions can also impact on

Table 3.1 Identified factors that impact on educational outcomes

Factor	Impact
Some of the factors identified that schools have no or little control over:	
Gender	Being male can lead to poorer outcomes, so we need to consider how we can better support boys to succeed in school, academic or otherwise.
Ethnicity	Being White British or Irish is a factor for poorer outcomes in education.
Age entering care	Entering care during secondary school makes poorer educational outcomes more likely.
Length of time in care	Being in care longer, generally, the better the outcomes (Sebba et al., 2015).

Factor	Impact
SEN	Having autism, a moderate learning difficulty, or severe or multiple learning difficulties, unsurprisingly, impacts negatively on educational outcomes.
Some identified factors where schools can have a positive impact:	
Prior attainment	A focus on progress is important, as prior attainment does not always reflect a CYP's ability. Having high expectations and making sure support is in place at the earliest opportunity can make a real difference. Beware of using 'flight paths' (computer-generated predictions based on prior attainment) to predict future attainment for CYP with social care involvement.
School mobility	A focus on maintaining school stability is important, as increased school moves impacts negatively on outcomes. Think carefully before considering managed moves, as this can potentially lead to a loss of learning due to the disruption of starting a new school and the time it takes to feel safe to learn again. School moves have an even greater impact on CYP who are not in care, especially in terms of progress at key stage 2 and attainment across all key stages (Sebba et al., 2015).
Type of school	Mainstream schools achieve the best outcomes. Attending a Pupil Referral Unit (PRU) can result in a 14-point lower grade difference in GCSEs when all other factors are accounted for (Sebba et al., 2015).
Exclusions	Permanent exclusions lead to changes of school and often result in a pupil moving to AP or a PRU. These both increase the chance of poorer educational outcomes. Fixed-term exclusions mean CYP miss learning time in school, and the sense of rejection can impact on relationships with school staff.
Ofsted grading of school	CiC should not be placed in schools that are not rated Good or Outstanding. Attainment 8 scores and access to the EBacc tend to be higher in Good and Outstanding schools, and progress is considerably higher than in Inadequate schools (DfE, 2018).
Then there are some factors where children's social care has a key role to play:	
In/out of borough	Whether a child is placed in a school in the borough in which they are cared for or out of borough has a variable impact. There may be less support available from the virtual school if a child is placed in another LA.
Number of care placement moves	There is a direct relationship between the number of care placements a child has and their educational outcomes, so supporting care placement stability is important (Sebba et al., 2015).
Strengths and Difficulties Questionnaires (SDQ)	All CiC should have an SDQ completed by their carer each year. Ideally, the school and young person (aged 11-plus) should also complete an SDQ to give a fuller picture of how the child is coping at home and school. The higher the SDQ score, the poorer the educational outcomes, but even a score that is slightly above average can impact outcomes (Sebba et al., 2015).

educational success. Thanks to The National Association of Virtual School Heads, the DfE and the National Consortium for Examination Results, VSH now have access to an invaluable database that combines education and social care data. This enables analysis of the data using numerous filters to further identify the factors that make the most difference. Many virtual schools have small cohort numbers, so the National Center for Education Research (NCER) reports enable comparisons of CYP with similar national profiles to provide a useful benchmark. This is especially helpful, given the variation in the needs of CiC – across all ages, abilities, ethnicities and care experiences.

The impact of trauma and attachment

Dr Gabor Maté, a clinical psychologist, defines trauma as follows:

> Trauma is a psychic wound that hardens you psychologically that then inter-feres with your ability to grow and develop. It pains you and now you're acting out of pain. It induces fear and now you're acting out of fear. So, without know-ing it, your whole life is regulated by fear and pain that you're trying to escape from in various ways. Trauma is not what happens to you, it's what happens inside you as a result of what happened to you.
>
> (Caparrotta, 2020)

A range of other factors are linked to a CYP experiencing ACEs that are much harder to quantify or measure, as each child will experience the impact of abuse, neglect and family disfunction differently. Schools are becoming increasingly aware of attachment and trauma, and how these impact on classroom learning. This chapter focuses on what is known as 'relational and developmental trauma', the complex trauma caused by abuse and neglect carried out by people the child relies on, usually caregivers and other fam-ily members. Schools need to understand that if a CYP has experienced relational trauma, it makes it much harder for them to feel safe with adults, especially those with whom they don't have an established relationship.

Developmental trauma is focused on the impact of the child's develop-ment, as a result of the complex trauma. Children's brains develop from the bot-tom up, starting from the brain stem and developing up to the limbic brain and the pre-frontal cortex. This simple model is the triune brain model (Figure 3.2).

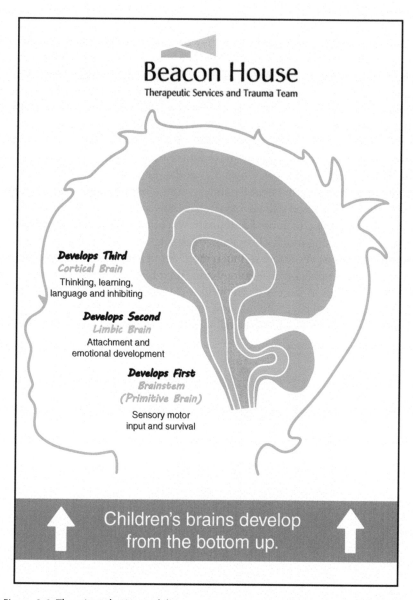

Figure 3.2 The triune brain model
(Beacon House, 2021)

The neurosequential model helps to explain the impact of trauma on learning. If a child has lived in fear, they often have an overdeveloped survival response in the lower part of the brain that has helped to keep them safe. This can present in school as hypervigilance; CYP might find themselves in a state of fight or flight more quickly or more often than others. The limbic brain helps to control emotions and our ability to form relationships, so this area often needs further support to help fill some of the interruptions a child has had due to their relational trauma. The pre-frontal cortex is key to learning, as this controls our executive functions and is the part of the brain that helps to control our stress response and emotional regulation. For CYP with trauma histories, the neural pathways to the pre-frontal cortex may still need strengthening and will be impacted by how safe a child feels in school.

The impact of attachment and trauma on participation and learning in school is becoming much clearer since research in this area has increased over recent years. We know so much more about how living with adversity in childhood impacts neurobiology and, therefore, on a child's ability to feel safe enough to access learning in a classroom environment. Dr Kim Golding, a clinical psychologist, developed a Pyramid of Need (Figure 3.3) (Golding and Hughes, 2012) to demonstrate the hierarchy of needs for a

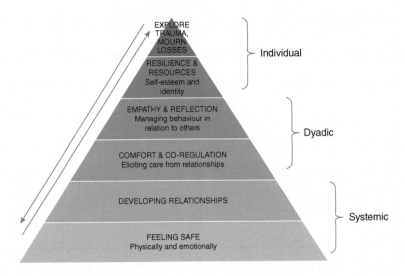

Figure 3.3 Pyramid of need
(Golding and Hughes, 2012)

child that has experienced relational trauma. Knowing where a child is on this should help inform the identified support needs and target setting. While this model was originally created for a therapeutic model known as Dyadic Developmental Psychotherapy (DDP), it is increasingly being applied in education settings.

It helps to think of the pyramid in terms of a 'graduated approach' (DfE and DoH, 2015, p. 100) for CYP who have experienced trauma. It also helps to consider which elements are about the systems in place (policies, procedures and environmental factors), which are dyadic and which are about the relationships a pupil has in place to achieve 'comfort and co-regulation' and 'empathy and reflection'. The top two levels are for when a child has the other levels in place and is then able to build their resilience and self-esteem. The top level, around addressing traumas and losses, is likely to be achieved through external therapeutic resources, but this can still be part of an education plan.

A child may move up and down the pyramid at different times, depending on circumstances in and out of school. Recognising where a CYP is on the pyramid can help determine the support needed at the time. For example, a CYP finding it hard to attend school may be feeling unsafe away from their carer or in a school setting. They may need further work done around relationships before admitting this, and changes can be made to the environmental factors causing a barrier. A CYP struggling with peer relationships may need more time receiving comfort from an adult, modelling kindness and empathy.

 REFLECTIVE ACTIVITY

When considering the needs of a CYP in education, how much attention is given to environmental factors?

How much importance is placed upon developing trusting relationships?

PEPs

The final section of this chapter will focus on the PEP. While PEPs are only for CiC, the focus in the SMART targets section will be applicable in target setting for CYP that have experienced relational and developmental

trauma. Those with an EHCP with a primary need linked to SEMH needs may well have a trauma history underlying their behavioural presentation. Dr Bruce Perry urges us to reframe our thinking: 'it is not what is wrong with you but what happened to you?' (Perry and Winfrey, 2021).

A PEP is part of a childcare plan. It brings together the CYP, their designated teacher in school, their carer and their social worker (and sometimes their birth parents, if appropriate) to discuss how best to meet their educational needs and help them achieve their aspirations. Due to the number of people involved in the creation of each PEP, it is little wonder that Ofsted described PEPs as variable:

> The quality seen by inspectors was variable. The standard of the plans was constrained by a variety of factors, including difficulties with electronic data systems and the inconsistent approach to holding face-to-face meetings. Most importantly, targets set for children and young people were not all sufficiently specific or challenging.
>
> (Ofsted, 2021, pp. 29–30)

This following section explores how we might reduce this variability and create PEPs to be proud of, that are a catalyst for improvement in educational outcomes. As mentioned, around half of CiCs will also have either an SEN support plan or an EHCP, so care needs to be taken to ensure duplication is avoided and targets are aligned. The DfE Statutory Guidance states this:

> The PEP is a record of the child's education and training. It should describe what needs to happen for a looked-after child to help them fulfil their potential and reflect, but not duplicate, any existing plans such as EHC plans.
>
> (DfE, 2018b, p. 15)

PEPs need to be much more than a form-filling exercise. They need to be a scaffold for a meaningful discussion between the CYP and their support network. They need to be specific in addressing their needs and reducing barriers to learning, enhancing all that is already in place and making sure the right support is provided at the right time. This means staff in schools leading on the PEPs need to understand the impact of relational and developmental trauma on participation in learning.

CYP voice in the PEP

The PEP needs to include the views of the CYP, so schools need to think about how best to do this. Many designated teachers enjoy spending some quality one-to-one time with a child; others delegate this part of the PEP to another member of staff who knows the child best, which often elicits the most honest responses. There should be a range of tools to gather views, including questionnaires, drawing options and general conversations. While it is important to have the views of the child present in the meeting, best practice involves the child being there, too, if they want this. Be careful if this means taking children out of lessons, as many don't like the stigma of being treated differently, and they shouldn't miss learning for the PEP.

 REFLECTIVE ACTIVITY

How do you gather the views of CYP?
Who is responsible for gathering views? How do you decide? What choice do CYP have in whom they speak to?
How do the views of CYP shape their education plans?

Mentalizing

Taking a 'mentalizing stance' (Figure 3.4) can help understand how the CYP feels about school. Mentalizing is about considering what might be in someone else's mind, considering what the world might be like from their perspective. Hearing from the child directly and their teachers, carers and social worker can help build a comprehensive picture of what school is like for them from different angles. A carer might notice certain days are harder to get them out of the door; one teacher may have a different experience than another teacher; or the child's social worker may be aware of past experiences and current situations that may impact the CYP. The PEP should be informed by the views of everyone, with the child at the centre.

Figure 3.4 The mentalizing stance

Mentalizing is thinking about what is going on in someone else's mind. It can also be called 'being mind-minded'. We need to imagine what school feels like for children and work out how we can improve it.

Promoting agency

One of the findings from the Rees Centre research on the educational outcomes of CiN (Sebba et al., 2015) was that those in the high-progress group had a greater sense of agency. The authors described examples of strong self-advocacy and persistence, and made direct recommendations to foster carers and professionals on how they could better support them:

> Listen a lot, a hell of a lot. Listen, because not enough people do that. I mean, there are a lot of kids out there that do need help, and they won't ask because they're too scared to, or they're too scared to get shut down. So, if a child is telling you they need help, you need to listen, and even if they're not telling you, ask questions. Ask them if they need help, because a lot of kids don't get asked that.

> (p. 29)

If a child feels confident to speak out, knowing they will be listened to and taken seriously, this helps not only to get the right support in place but to build agency too.

PEPs and EHCPs

Around half (55.7%) of CiC have an EHCP or SEN support plan (DfE, 2021). It is important that these plans, including their targets and outcomes, are aligned with the PEP. The PEP should not simply duplicate the SEN support or EHCP but should further enhance it. The PEP should be an opportunity to revisit other plans, the latest school report, attendance information and assessment data, to form a clear oversight of how the CYP is doing. It is also an opportunity to clarify how SEND funding and the pupil premium plus (an enhanced amount of pupil premium for CiC and previously LAC) (DfE, 2021c) are being used already and what impact this is having. The designated teacher should come to the PEP meeting with a clear understanding of the strengths and areas for development to be discussed in the meeting.

In my LA, we ask schools to review key documentation and information available before they come to the PEP meeting (Table 3.2). This provides an

Table 3.2 North Tyneside LA pre-PEP checklist for schools

Data	To check
Current PEP / previous PEP	Review what was agreed at last meeting; check goals and whether CYP is on track to achieve them. Are they still relevant?
CYP views for this term's PEP	Are there any issues raised that need taking to the meeting or anything that needs clarifying before the meeting? What are their future aspirations? How can they be supported to achieve them?
Recent school report	Strongest subjects, subjects where issues have been raised, current grades, predicted grades or target grades – are the target grades aspirational enough? Any teachers to seek updates or clarification from before meeting?
SEN – EHCP / SEN support plan	How effective is the current support? Does it have a positive impact? Are targets being met? What are the key areas of focus – link to goals/actions in PEP. Is support sitting at the right level – too little or too much support in place? Does the CYP still need an EHCP or can needs be met through SEN support? Does a statutory assessment need to take place?

(Continued)

Table 3.2 (Continued) North Tyneside LA pre-PEP checklist for schools

Data	To check
Data tracking reports	Check whether age-related expectations are met, progress is made, prior attainment compared to current attainment, and flight paths are aspirational enough; gaps in knowledge; areas where further assessment may be needed.
Attendance record	95% or above, PA, attendance patterns, punctuality, exclusions and term-time holidays?
Behaviour record	Rewards/incentives versus sanctions/consequences, any patterns/issues in particular classes/times of day, decline/improvements and reasons why.
Strengths and Difficulties Questionnaire (further information later)	Who has access to the carer version? Does the school complete their version? Any concerns raised? Has bullying been reported? Impact on classroom learning? Peer relationships?
Pupil premium plus (up to £2,345 per pupil – further information later)	How has funding been used and with what impact? Has all of it been allocated? Anything in pupil views that needs funding?

opportunity to reflect on how the CYP is doing and what may need further discussion in the PEP meeting.

The pupil premium plus

The pupil premium is for disadvantaged CYP entitled to free school meals (FSM). Pupil premium has been available since 2011, and most schools have well-developed pupil premium strategies published on their website, stating how the funding has been used and the impact it has had on outcomes. There is another cohort of CYP that benefits from the enhanced pupil premium plus (PP+). For CiC, this funding is managed and distributed to schools by the VSH for the LA that has the care responsibility for them. Each VSH will have their own pupil premium policy that determines how this funding is distributed, and most will retain some of the funding to enhance the offer from the virtual school. In many virtual schools, a proportion is retained to provide therapeutic interventions, additional teaching support and crisis support as and when needed. It is important to include details of how the funding has been used and the impact it has had in the PEP.

CYP who were previously looked after and have secured permanency through adoption, a Special Guardianship Order or a Child Arrangement Order, are also eligible for the PP+, but caregivers must self-declare their child's status to the school for the school to be able to access this funding. Many schools now include this in their admissions forms, but it is the responsibility of the caregivers to provide evidence of the legal status of the child. Schools add these pupils to the autumn school census then receive the funding in the next financial year. Although the funding is not ring-fenced, there is an expectation that funding is individualised to meet the needs of previously looked after pupils.

'The PP+ can be used to facilitate a wide range of educational support for looked after and previously looked after children. Interventions supported by pupil premium must be evidence-based and in the child's best interests' (DfE, 2018b).

Target setting in the PEP

Once the needs have been clearly identified, short-term and long-term targets need to be set within the PEP meeting. The CYP and their network need to understand these targets, so avoid using language and acronyms that others will not understand. Make it clear who will deliver on the target and what the timescales are for achieving the target outcome. CYP and their caregivers and social workers can set targets because everyone has a role to play in improving the educational outcomes of CiC.

SMART targets in PEPs

Think about what will make the most significant difference to educational outcomes for the individual CYP based on all the available information

77

and the views of everyone, including the child and their network. Thinking specifically about the needs of CYP that have experienced trauma, the focus should be on the needs identified in the Pyramid of Needs (Golding and Hughes, 2012, p. 123) (Figure 3.3), alongside learning needs.

This may include targets that address the following:

- Helping them to feel safe in school
- Developing positive relationships with staff and CYP
- Meeting any unmet needs, including social, emotional and academic
- Filling gaps in knowledge and understanding
- Accelerating progress beyond expectations
- Meeting the aspirations of the child and their network
- Maintaining stability
- Transitioning to the next stage/phase

SMART target examples

To help consider what these might look like, we will consider Curtis, a year 8 boy:

Curtis's views

When Curtis was asked if there was anything he was worried about when his designated teacher was asking his views for his PEP, he responded, 'Nothing'. She couldn't get him to say any more.

The PEP meeting

At the PEP meeting, his designated teacher, social worker and foster carer spoke about what was currently happening in Curtis's life and how it might impact him at school (Figures 3.5, 3.6 and 3.7).

'Curtis is finding it hard to focus on learning because he has recently been told by his social worker that his mum has been hurt by his stepdad again. He told her he is worried his stepdad might come to school to hurt him too, like he did when he lived at home. His teacher has noticed he is now wary of speaking to teachers when he is worried.'

Figure 3.5 Quote from Curtis's designated teacher

'His teachers have noticed he spends the day watching out the windows and seems terrified anytime someone enters the classroom. He has told me that when a teacher shouts, he is reminded of what life was like when he lived at home. His teacher shared that he has been known to hide under the table in the classroom. I've been told he is falling behind his peers and that he makes excuses not to do his work, especially when they are doing maths. It is hard to get him to complete his maths homework.'

Figure 3.6 Quote from Curtis's foster carer

'I wonder if he can't concentrate on any learning because he is worried about his mum and wishes he was still at home to look after her. She knows he feels to blame for his mum getting hurt because he told his teacher what had happened at home and she contacted children's services.'

Figure 3.7 Quote from Curtis's social worker

This example demonstrates the importance of the PEP being completed within a meeting, as different people in the CYP's network hold useful information that helps to make sense of what is going on for Curtis at the moment. Following the discussion, it becomes clearer what issues need to be addressed to help Curtis access learning.

- Curtis does not feel safe in school (he is worried his stepdad will get into the building), especially when teachers shout
- He is in a heightened state of fear following an assault on his mother by his stepdad
- Curtis finds it hard to trust adults
- Curtis is falling behind academically, particularly in maths

Following (Tables 3.3, 3.4, 3.5 and 3.6) is a range of targets that could be used to support Curtis. The PEP needs to clarify who is responsible for delivering on the target and what the timescale are when it will happen. Everyone has a role to play in improving the outcomes of CiC.

Table 3.3 Priority 1: feeling safe

Aim	SMART target	Measure of success
Create a sense of safety in school.	Complete a safety tour of the school with Curtis within the next two weeks, including access arrangements into school, who is on duty, fire exits and first-aiders. This could be done with foster carer to reinforce safety messages about school.	Curtis feels safer in school and is better able to access classroom learning.
Help a pupil feel safe to learn.	Identify preferred seat in classroom where Curtis feels safest within the next two weeks.	Curtis's level of hypervigilance reduces. Curtis is more focused on learning.
Have a clear 'exit from the classroom' strategy for times when Curtis feels overwhelmed.	Formulate an exit strategy with Curtis and his key adult that identifies a safe place to go to when feeling overwhelmed. To be completed within six weeks and reviewed before next PEP meeting.	Curtis can use the exit strategy successfully and feels more confident in managing when feeling overwhelmed.
Prepare Curtis for any changes in the day to reduce anxiety.	Implement a two-minute check-in with Curtis at the start of each day with his key adult.	Curtis is aware of any changes and feels less anxious and better prepared for the day.

Aim	SMART target	Measure of success
Create a safe and calm environment.	Develop and implement a no-shouting policy within the next six months. Training for school staff?	Curtis will less likely be triggered by adults raising their voices and will feel that adults are in control of themselves and can keep CYP safe.
Promote safe relationships within school.	Deliver three lessons on safe relationships through SRE curriculum over the next term.	Curtis and other children will develop an understanding of what makes relationships safe.

Table 3.4 Priority 2: sensory regulation

Aim	SMART target	Measure of success
Help to reduce Curtis's emotional arousal level at times of stress.	To organise, set up and devise a sensory break at agreed times during the day to reduce risk of arousal levels increasing.	Curtis can remain within a comfortable arousal state for most of the day.
Provide strategies to help maintain low arousal levels.	To make, prepare and set up a calm box with Curtis, containing five tools that can be used to help Curtis create a sense of calm. This could include a transitional object from home.	Curtis will use the calm box when prompted by an adult and eventually be able to use strategies independently.
Better understand Curtis's sensory needs.	To undertake a sensory assessment with an educational psychologist or occupational therapist to better understand Curtis's sensory needs.	Curtis will have his sensory needs recognised, and support can be put in place to help with sensory regulation.
Better understand Curtis's triggers and calmers.	To complete a 'states continuum' with Curtis's key adult to better understand his emotional states and presentation during those states. To be completed within four weeks. Ask foster carer to do the same for home.	Curtis has greater awareness of what takes him into heightened state of arousal and how best to calm him. Strategies used at home and school become more aligned.
Help Curtis better understand his stress response system.	To provide Curtis with a five-session course in psychoeducation by a teacher from the virtual school, to explain and to help him understand his stress response system.	Curtis better understands his brain and the fight, flight or freeze response. He understands how to calm himself and some fear is removed.

81

Table 3.5 Priority 3: developing relationships

Aim	SMART target	Measure of success
Identify Curtis's key attachment figures.	Social worker to schedule and lead a rope hold assessment (this is a picture of a person abseiling, and Curtis is asked to add who he would have holding the rope at the top of the cliff). The social worker could complete this.	School staff better understand Curtis's attachments and who he trusts and considers reliable. If a child struggles to think of someone, this shows the need to develop attachments with adults.
Develop a trusting relationship with a key adult in school.	Designated teacher to identify a suitable key adult and timetable relationship-building sessions for 15 to 20 minutes, 3 times a week.	Curtis seeks out the key adult when he needs support in school.
Develop a relationship with class/subject teacher.	Teacher to implement the ten-by-two approach to develop a relationship with Curtis. (This means finding two minutes a day for ten days to chat with Curtis and get to know him better.)	Curtis feels more comfortable with member of staff and starts to build trust.
Have member of SLT get to know Curtis better to understand ways school systems may need adapting.	Deputy head to provide 30 minutes a week for half a term to play a game with Curtis and find out more about his experience of school.	Curtis feels valued and safer in school.
Provide flexible support for when Curtis needs it.	Key adult to implement a check-in with Curtis twice a day and be readily available when needed.	Curtis feels safer as he knows a key adult is looking out for him and feels able to seek help when needed.

Table 3.6 Priority 4: filling gaps in knowledge

Aim	SMART target	Measure of success
Better understand gaps in knowledge.	Complete maths assessment to identify gaps in knowledge and provide additional support to help fill gaps.	Curtis can understand aspects of maths causing difficulties, and his confidence increases.
Build confidence in maths.	Pre-teach and explain a maths topic so Curtis feels more confident in class and can answer questions and help others.	Curtis feels less anxious about maths and can contribute during the lesson.

Aim	SMART target	Measure of success
Get some basics in place.	Memorise and recite 4- and 6-times tables within the next 3 weeks, with support from foster carer.	Curtis finds it quicker and easier to complete maths tasks, and his confidence increases.
Make maths fun.	Produce a weekly maths puzzle for Curtis based on something he is interested in.	Curtis is given some challenge and starts to build a connection with the maths teacher.
Build self-belief in maths.	Produce a list of ten maths affirmations for Curtis to learn at home to help change his mindset about maths.	Curtis starts to believe he is able to become a better mathematician and becomes more willing to try to do maths problems rather than give up so quickly.

The lives of CiC are complex, and they need a higher level of scrutiny and understanding than other CYP to enable them to achieve in education. CYP that have been previously looked after, while they do not have the requirement of a PEP, do have additional needs linked to prior experiences and the benefit of the PP+. CiN and those on a CPP make up a much larger cohort within some schools, and their needs may need to be looked at more closely through a trauma lens.

Chapter summary

1   There is a need to align EHCPs/SEN support plans with PEPs for CiC.
2   The virtual school can support with advice and information for CiC and previously LAC. The new role around CiN can support schools to think more systemically about a graduated response to trauma.
3   There are a range of factors that impact on educational outcomes for CYP that have experienced LA care. These include school stability, exclusions, prior attainment, SEND needs and care factors, such as the number of placement moves and length of time in care.
4   Developmental and relational trauma is another factor that impacts on learning, and a wider cohort of CYP may have experienced this in the CiN group. Schools need to place a high importance on safety and relationships to enable these CYP to access learning successfully.

5   The voices of CYP should be central to planning and target setting. It is difficult for some CYP to share their views. The views from their network can help understand their perspective by using a mentalizing approach.

Recommended reading

Statutory guidance

Department for Education (DfE) (2018a) *The designated teacher for looked after and previously looked-after children: Statutory guidance on their roles and responsibilities.* London: DfE.

DfE (2018b) *Promoting the education of looked after children and previously looked after children: Statutory guidance for local authorities.* London: DfE.

DfE (2021) *Promoting the education of children with a social worker. Virtual School Head role extension.* London: DfE.

Books

Bombèr, L.M. (2007) *Inside I'm hurting: Practical strategies for supporting children with attachment difficulties in schools.* London: Worth Publishing Ltd.

Bombèr, L.M. (2020) *Know me to teach me: Differentiated discipline for those recovering from adverse childhood experiences.* London: Worth Publishing Ltd

De Thierry, B. (2016) *The simple guide to child trauma: What it is and how to help.* London: Jessica Kingsley Publishers.

Golding, K., Bombèr, L.M. and Phillips, S. (2020) *Working with relational trauma in schools: An educator's guide to using dyadic developmental psychotherapy in schools.* London: Jessica Kingsley Publishers.

Research

Berridge, D. et al. (2020) *Children in Need and Children in Care: Educational Attainment and Progress.* The Rees Centre, Oxford: Oxford University. Raija, P. and Välivaara, C. (2018) 'Educational intervention planning for children in foster care in Finland: A case study', *Education Inquiry*, 9(2), pp. 237–246.

Sebba, J. et al. (2015) *The educational progress of looked after children in England: Linking care and educational data.* The Rees Centre, Oxford: Oxford University.

Useful websites

Beacon House (https://beaconhouse.org.uk/resources/): Provides freely available resources to support children who have experienced trauma and adversity.

Flipping your lid (https://www.treeforttherapy.com/blog/flipping-your-lid): Provides information about the emotional states (arousal) continuum by Dr Bruce Perry.

References

Beacon House (2021) *Children's brains develop from the bottom up.* Available at: https://beaconhouse.org.uk/wp-content/uploads/2019/09/3-stages-of-brain-development-2.jpg (Accessed: 1 December 2021).

Berridge, D., Luke, N., Sebba, J., Strand, S., Cartwright, M., Staples, E., McGrath-Lone, L., Ward, J. and O'Higgins, A. (2020) *Children in need and children in care: Educational attainment and progress.* Bristol: University of Bristol.

Caparrotta, M. (2020) *Dr Gabor Maté on childhood trauma, The real cause of anxiety and our 'insane' culture*. Human Window. Available at: https//humanwindow.com/dr-gabor-mate-interview-childhood-trauma-anxiety-culture/ (Accessed: 25 November 2021).

Children and Families Act (CAFA) 2014, s.99. Available at: https://www.legislation.gov.uk/ukpga/2014/6/contents/enacted (Accessed: 25 November 2021).

Department for Education (DfE) and Department of Health (DoH) (2015) *Special educational needs and disability code of practice: 0 to 25 years Statutory guidance for organisations which work with and support children and young people who have special educational needs or disabilities*. London: DfE.

DfE (2018a) *Promoting the education of looked after children and previously looked after children: Statutory guidance for local authorities*. London: DfE.

DfE (2018b) *The designated teacher for looked after and previously looked-after children: Statutory guidance on their roles and responsibilities*. London: DfE.

DfE (2021a) *Promoting the education of children with a social worker Virtual School Head role extension*. London: DfE.

DfE (2021b) *Outcomes for children in need, including children looked after by local authorities in England*. Available at: https://explore-education-statistics.service.gov.uk/find-statistics/outcomes-for-children-in-need-including-children-looked-after-by-local-authorities-in-england/2020 (Accessed: 25 November 2021).

DfE (2021c) *Guidance pupil premium*. Available at: https//www.gov.uk/government/publications/pupil-premuim/pupil-premium (Accessed: 25 November 2021).

Golding, K. and Hughes, D. (2012) *Creating loving attachments: Parenting with PACE to nurture confidence and security in the troubled child*. London: Jessica Kingsley Publishers.

Ofsted (2021) *School inspection handbook*. Available at: https://www.gov.uk/government/publications/school-inspection-handbook-eif/school-inspection-handbook (Accessed: 9 December 2021).

Perry, B. and Winfrey, O. (2021) *What Happened to you? Conversations on trauma, resilience, and healing.* London: Bluebird.

Sebba, J. et al. (2015) *The educational progress of looked after children in England: Linking care and educational data.* The Rees Centre, Oxford: Oxford University.

Battling to be heard
The impact on families
Catherine Landucci

4

This chapter shares in-depth conversations with three caregivers of CYP with SEND. Their experiences of co-production across the agencies of education, health and children's social care are explored and discussed. The extent to which the caregivers were listened and involved in the target setting varied, mostly dependent on the child's needs. Through the conversations, key themes emerged and are presented within the chapter.

The challenges to co-production with caregivers

The caregivers reflected on the limitations to co-producing provision and practice for their children (Table 4.1).

Table 4.1 Challenges to co-production

Overarching theme	Detail
Access to resources	Caregivers were told that it was harder to justify allocating support because their child didn't disrupt other children's learning. Two caregivers were informed that if their child would only hurt other children, they would get support.
Private financing	Many children were unable to access resources due to lack of funding in school or needed crisis support due to lengthy waiting times in pressurised health services. Therefore, caregivers who could afford to pay for private assessments for dyslexia and educational psychologist assessments for autism did so. Others financed specialist tutors whose focus was to try and enable children to catch up with the expectations and pressures of the national curriculum.

DOI: 10.4324/9781003261506-5

Overarching theme	Detail
Shaming	Some caregivers said they felt shamed by educational professionals and education welfare officers. Children were described as lazy or needing to change their behaviour despite huge neurodiverse differences. Caregivers were told to be stronger and that they needed to support their children to be more independent when they were at breaking point trying to get their child's needs met.
Inadequate school systems and policies for SEMH needs	School systems and policies do not account for nor accommodate meeting SEMH needs. Behaviour systems were not fit to support children with trauma or anxiety. Some staff were unwilling or unskilled to think about behaviour as anything other than a bad choice made by the child, so they were not able to put in place strategies and provision that would make a difference and meet the need.
Lack of training for school staff for learning needs	Only two caregivers said that the schools were able to meet their child's learning needs. Dyslexia seemed to baffle school staff, and parents found themselves trying to bridge the gap by funding private tuition.
Work in education enabled better advocacy	Caregivers who worked in education and knew what should be available were better able to advocate for their child to receive what they needed – although this wasn't always the case.
Identification of need driven by parental pressure	Only one caregiver had experienced the school instigating meetings and identifying needs. Others had to request meetings and push to have their child's needs met.
Parental guilt	A sense of responsibility was evident with all caregivers. It was their role to advocate and push for support. Few were clear that it was the school's job to be leading on their children's provision and education. Their comments included 'I dropped the ball'; 'I wanted to pretend everything was ok, I felt ashamed that I couldn't get her to school'; and 'I didn't have the knowledge'.

Case study 1: Shushma and Layla

Shushma adopted Layla, having fostered her from birth. Layla has a diagnosis of cystic fibrosis, foetal alcohol spectrum disorder (FASD) and, more recently, autism. Shushma decided to homeschool due to the challenges encountered in having their voices heard.

Effective multidisciplinary response

When Layla started school, due to her complex needs and feeding peg, she was allocated a full-time one-to-one, who received training and support from the Great Ormond Street Hospital nurses, the Physical and Sensory Team, and the community nurse. A homeschool communication book communicated her feeds, toileting and any behaviour issues.

Barriers to thriving

Shushma was invited to termly meetings to review the provision in place. Still, while there was a focus on enabling Layla to physically be in school, there was no understanding of supporting a child with FASD to thrive. 'The training was enabling her to be in the building – not to overcome her barriers to learning'. The LA's educational psychologist was called upon to advise, but they didn't have an assessment to match her difficulties.

The expert was me

The school observed Layla could speak and concluded she didn't need visuals. Yet without them, she struggled to comprehend language. Shushma reflected, 'the expert was me'. Often, teachers' fixed ideas didn't match the information given to Shushma by the GOSH team of experts, and she felt it was a struggle to get them to listen.

 REFLECTIVE ACTIVITY

During the conversation, Shushma reflected, 'When you champion your child's needs, some professionals can take it as a personal affront, or perhaps don't feel they can say they don't know the answers'.

How comfortable would you be to say to a caregiver you know little about their child's needs?

Target setting

Targets set were not achievable. The expectations didn't match Layla's physical or emotional capabilities. Nor did they consider her aspirations and loves – dancing, singing and cooking. Toileting was their main focus but so was food, as she wouldn't eat at school. What wasn't being understood was that Layla was so stressed and dysregulated. She would tip into shame with every mistake made, and that was why she wouldn't eat.

Shaming

In an hour-long meeting with the LA's Physical Needs Team, focusing solely on Layla's toileting, Shushma recalls her daughter being labelled 'lazy'. She was advised to be stronger and firmer, and to better support the school's focus on independent toileting. Leaving that meeting shamed and frustrated, she knew that her daughter's low muscle tone and emotional state meant she wasn't ready for what they were asking. She contacted the occupational therapist and psychologist assigned to Layla. They concurred that she definitely wasn't ready for independent toileting.

FASD – the lesser-known SEND

Shushma has found there isn't a great deal of knowledge about FASD, so when she advocated for what Layla actually needed, 'Everyone thought I was mad. When Layla was diagnosed with autism, it got attention. FASD didn't do the trick'. Autism was easier for the team to understand.

Lockdown and homeschooling

Lockdown presented an opportunity to see what homeschooling looked like for Layla and her family. It was a game changer. Eating was no longer problematic, and Shushma, taking a more neurodevelopmental approach, approached Layla's education differently. Teaching toileting through play took the stress and shame away. Using cooking, singing and dancing to teach maths enabled her to develop and learn.

Case study 2: Julie and Emma

This case study shares the voice of Julie as she reflects on her daughters' dyslexia, which, when not acknowledged, led to school phobia and social anxiety diagnosis. Not being listened to resulted in huge pressure on the family, leading to Julie feeling shame and anxiety. Julie shared that she was prescribed anxiety medication to manage the stress.

Sunshine child: the early years

Emma went from being a happy sunshine child to one with significant anxiety by year 2 of school and was struggling to read and write:

> I was inexperienced and worried about being judged, so minimised it and hoped it would go away. Emma's dad is dyslexic and I knew I had the traits too. I managed to get a meeting with the SENCO. She told me that funding was tight and that if she was a naughtier child and hurt other children, she would get more help. That was the wakeup call that the SENCO wasn't going to solve things.

Junior and secondary school

They decided to change junior schools, where Emma was informally assessed as having dyslexic traits. She was given specialist one-to-one teaching twice a week and began to make progress. Emma achieved very good SAT scores for English, which Julie believes did her no favours in secondary school, as she was put in a high set for English.

Emma's anxiety hit the roof. The homework was overwhelming and unachievable. She was suffering from the pressure, so I asked for a meeting with the SENCO and was told Emma didn't have dyslexia, she was just anxious.

By then, the pressure and anxiety had made her so ill she had lost weight and was physically sick most days, but the school told Julie to bring her in regardless.

Dyslexia Institute

Julie arranged a private assessment from the Dyslexia Institute. They wrote a detailed report confirming a diagnosis of dyslexia, which Julie took to the school. The school refused to look at it, stating that they didn't recognise a private report.

No compassion, no kindness

Emma was ill so often that Julie continuously went to the GP for sick notes. Once, she was diagnosed with an anxiety-induced tracheitis cough, caused by the stress of going to school. Yet they insisted she still came in – and when she coughed, she was told to stop. Julie contacted Parent Partnership, who attended meetings.

> It was a way of legally trying to cover myself. I felt like no one was there for me or thinking about my child – no compassion, no kindness. Even my friends would tell me, 'You're not strong enough, you need to be stronger'.

The family engaged in family therapy, and Emma was eventually allocated an anxiety specialist, but even that didn't meet the approval of the school, as the SENCO advised Julie not to take Emma to the sessions. Social anxiety set in for Emma, and her parents felt under pressure to ensure being off school was not 'fun' – no watching TV or going to shops.

Reintegration plan – some success at last

Finally, the school put together a reintegration plan – a reduced timetable for three months. Emma walked to school independently and would come home at lunchtime. It was a seismic change. However, Christmas came, and the school told Julie that they were unwilling to continue with the reduced timetable, insisting she returned full-time in the new year.

End of reasonable adjustments – you just have to get her here

Emma tried to return to school but couldn't do it. Julie was forcing her to get dressed, and Emma was shaking and crying. Despite pleading with the school, Emma recalled that the education welfare officer reiterated, "you just have to get her here'. I had to not be a weak mother. The pressure was so great I went to the doctor in desperation, who put me on anti-anxiety medication to cope'.

The last day Emma attended that school, her dad took her in. He said he felt like he was abducting her. People were staring at him trying to drag her in. He rang the school and said, 'I need help'. He was told, 'we can't touch her, but the SENCO will come out to the playground'. Emma swore at the SENCO and then ran out of the school grounds.

 REFLECTIVE ACTIVITY

When Emma displayed physical manifestations of stress, what could the school have done differently?

Hospital, Home Tuition Team and diagnosis of school phobia and social anxiety

A multidisciplinary professional meeting was organised, and Julie managed to get Emma to attend. During the meeting, she got up and walked out.

It transpired that she had seen the SENCO rolling her eyes. The doctor from Child and Adolescent Mental Health Services (CAMHS) had seen it, too, and was appalled.

Emma was then referred to the hospital Home Tuition Team, having finally been diagnosed with school phobia and social anxiety. It was run in the local library, teaching core subjects for a couple of hours three times a week. The library was Emma's safe space.

Application for statutory assessment

Meanwhile, Julie was trying to put together an application for an education, health and care needs assessment. She paid a SENCO to help put it together, but the LA rejected it. Despite Emma remaining on roll at the secondary school, they wouldn't support the application at all. In the end, the doctor from CAMHS wrote a letter of support, co-produced with Julie. 'At last, people were understanding that I knew what she needed'.

New beginnings

Emma was awarded a statement of SEN, and people started listening, wanting to hear what she felt and needed. Emma was allocated a place in a different mainstream school through the statement of SEN. Since year 8, she hadn't been regularly in school, and Julie knew it wasn't the right setting for her, but she joined year 11. It was alright for a few weeks, but this happened:

> One day she just ripped up her blazer and ran off. It all blew up! I knew it would. At every meeting, I'd be realistic and say it how I saw it, but it came across that I was just being negative.

Emma was out of school again. Julie felt strongly that she needed a specialist provision to survive and thrive. She found a school that catered for young people with SEMH, autism and learning difficulties, or those at risk of exclusion. It was a fight to get the LA to agree to this. Even the head of that school said they didn't usually have students with Emma's needs. Yet they gave her a place, and she thrived. Her mother reflected, 'It was a total sea change. The school couldn't be more supportive; the shame was gone'. At a professionals' meeting, the relief that her daughter was getting what she needed overwhelmed Julie. 'The CAMHS representative came over and apologised that they hadn't known how to help. It meant a lot'.

> I later found out the SENCO who had been so cold with us had a daughter with the same needs. Every meeting we had was so official. I will never understand why she couldn't have sat me down with a cup of tea and made me feel like I wasn't the worst parent. In reality, I knew better than any of them. It was common sense, kindness and understanding; a bit of humanity that was needed.

 REFLECTIVE ACTIVITY

What, if any, reasons would there be to disregard assessments from professionals external to the school?

Is there a role for education welfare officers to investigate if there are unidentified special educational needs or disabilities?

Case study 3: Florence and Noah

Florence fosters a child, Noah, who is brave and courageous. As a small child, what happened to him had hardwired his brain to survive. None of his behaviours were naughty. They were a result of not being able to engage the thinking part of his brain. Instead, he saw threat everywhere, triggering the fight, flight and freeze responses. Noah's dangerous behaviour escalated to a point where he received a fixed-term exclusion. While a robust positive BSP had been thought through and the strategies Florence said had worked at home were included, the school didn't adopt them. In fact, the plan remained in the care of the class teacher and wasn't shared with the support staff or wider staff members.

Shaming

When Noah was in year 4, Florence was receiving behaviour updates almost daily – a list of everything he was doing wrong. They were managing a highly dysregulated child at home, whose deep-set trauma and flashbacks were a perpetual trigger for him. He wasn't coping at all in school or in any setting. She also heard from other caregivers that they'd seen Noah distressed around the school – once curled in a foetal position in the playground.

Some made their judgement clear through a caregivers' WhatsApp group that his behaviour at school was unacceptable and that Florence should be doing something about it. This made the playground an incredibly intimidating place at pickup. One afternoon, collecting him to take him for contact with his birth family, a regular supply teacher publicly shamed him in the playground, saying his behaviour that day had caused the class to be late in being dismissed. In truth, she was very stressed. The whole class had been so loud and out of her control, the parents could hear it outside. Florence later learned that on a day when she had been assured additional support would be allocated as she knew he would struggle, he had actually been sent out of class twice because of his behaviour; he wasn't coping.

Puzzling it out

There was very little work in any of his books at a 'book look'. When Florence asked if this was because his behaviour prevented him from accessing the learning, she was told that it wasn't the school's policy to record every lesson. Concerned that if there was no evidence of learning in his books, how could there be evidence of any academic challenges, Florence asked to see the head teacher.

The headteacher was brilliant, listening to her concerns and thoughtfully responding. She explained that they had already identified a need to address this area and agreed that Noah needed more opportunities to practise writing.

Backlash

Changes did happen. One month after his original exclusion, and subsequent exclusion from after-school provision for dangerous behaviour, a school newsletter introduced an upcoming homework task (Figure 4.1). This homework (Figure 4.2) tipped the scales in levels of stress in their home.

> When completing their shared story writing this week, the children have been encouraged to include the various grammar aspects and language features that we have been focusing on:
>
> - Fronted adverbials
> - Relative clauses
> - Expanded noun phrases
> - Possessive apostrophes
> - Speech

Figure 4.1 Newsletter extract: context to the task

> This week, we have completed some shared story writing. One focus has been to punctuate speech correctly. This week's homework task is to write a story that includes dialogue between at least two characters. This task is a long piece of writing. Your story must include the following:
>
> - A beginning (not starting with 'One sunny day . . .' or 'Once upon a time . . .')
> - Exciting events
> - The language features/grammar on the first page of the newsletter
>
> This story can be any genre you choose and must include original characters. You cannot use characters that already exist. Make sure to include detailed setting descriptions to really set the scene.

Figure 4.2 Homework: English task

What followed is documented in emails to and from the class teacher (names have been changed) (Figure 4.3 and Figure 4.4):

Hi Mrs Smith,

I'm having a hard time with the homework this week, and for the 5th time today, Noah has stormed upstairs and is banging away. We have spent a long time yesterday and today with the plot and planning the characters. Now he's onto the actual writing and his resilience as you know is minimal at the best of times.

Can you clarify how long you expect children to spend on the writing task? I wonder if it would be possible for writing tasks to have a framework around them or a specific focus. It's a lot for a child like Noah to try to generate a story in one homework session with a detailed setting, exciting events, fronted adverbials, direct speech and expanded noun phrases. It is a huge change in the style of homework he's been asked to do up till now. For it not to take over the entire weekend and cause high levels of stress, he would need a bit more structure around the task.

Figure 4.3 Email 1: Florence to teacher

Hi Florence,

The long writing task aims to consolidate our learning in class. The children find it quite easy to include a relative clause in class as it is just adding information to a character. Similarly, starting sentences with fronted adverbials has become second nature when we write stories, so it isn't designed to be a challenge for the children, simply consolidating classroom learning independently. For a story in Year 4, we would expect a beginning, build up, problem, resolution, ending. Noah can structure his story into these 5 paragraphs.

I have already received several stories through Google Docs, which motivates some children more than handwriting the story for homework. If Noah spent 15 minutes each day on his story, he would complete the story by Wednesday. He might find it easier to write out about 5 sentences for the beginning paragraph. Then go back and see if he can fit in a relative clause in that paragraph. Then on Saturday when he is writing his build up, again, he could write out 5 sentences. Then go back and see where he can fit in a fronted adverbial. On Sunday, he could write his problem, focusing on speech. And so on. Writing out a checklist like this might help him to see the progression of his work broken down into bite sized, achievable chunks.

Figure 4.4 Email 2: teacher to Florence

Dear Mrs Smith,

Since Friday, I have broken it down by thinking through and creating a story mountain with him to follow. He wouldn't have been ready to start writing on Friday evening as he needs time to process his thoughts and the requirements, plus he's shattered from coping all day at school. Today he has written a lot, which will be edited tomorrow – but as you know he is struggling at the moment, and it has caused huge episodes of crisis.

We're contending with overwhelming behaviours already. You're right, he does understand all the grammatical elements asked for and can include them. It's great that other children have already submitted stories but, I'm asking for more support with a homework task for Noah – be it that he writes the start of a story with all those elements, or writes a setting, or writes a dialogue. He just needs something that will be more manageable for him – as a child who is working towards age related expectations with significant emotional barriers to learning.

He will give in a story that he has worked really hard on Wednesday. I am asking that in future, some differentiation is made so the effort needed for him to complete his homework matches that of someone who doesn't have his barriers to learning.

Figure 4.5 Email 3: Florence to teacher

Noah's teacher was aware of the stress levels at home. Her response showed no compassion or understanding. It was enough to tip Florence into despair.

She didn't receive a response to that last email, so she sent a follow-up asking if the teacher had had a chance to think about it. She got this response, and it nearly broke her.

Hi Florence,

I spoke with the headteacher regarding Noah's homework. We don't want to lower the expectation for him as he rises to the challenge in class. As long as he is trying his best and submits what he has done, I don't mind if every aspect isn't covered in full detail. Some children just included relative clauses and spoke to me when they submitted it saying they found it tricky to include fronted adverbials. This is absolutely fine, because now they know it is something they can work on as a target. It doesn't have to be his 'best piece' by any means, as I understand that writing at home is different to writing at school, but I do want him to take accountability and responsibility for his writing as I don't want his progress to slow down.

The issues

He rose to the challenge in class. Yet there was no evidence of this in his book, nor the Google Drive, that this was the case. At home, they were trying to support a child already at risk of exclusion not just from school but clubs too, isolated by his behaviour in class, dysregulated by PTSD flashbacks and in a constant state of fight or flight. 'But', Florence recalled, 'Apparently, he should take accountability and responsibility for his writing and be able to sit down for 15 mins a day to write a creative tale with no support or plan. I felt hopeless. We were at capacity at home'.

The change

Florence felt totally let down by the school. She had trusted that the head knew their situation well enough and had felt shocked that they had been in agreement. Picking Noah up from school the next day, the head said, 'Hi, is everything ok?' Florence started crying. She got someone to scoop up Noah and take him to the office and took her to a room inside. Florence explained how the homework situation had been the last straw. The head didn't know anything about it. She listened and gave all the reassurance Florence needed, and things changed from thereon.

The class teacher left the school the following month. Since that time, Florence has always felt heard and able to advocate. Noah's next teacher, who had him for two years thereafter, was extraordinarily perceptive and thoughtful, enabling him to feel safe and capable. The targets and subsequent provision that was put in place made the difference to Noah's ability to be in school safely, be regulated enough to access the teaching, make and sustain friendships, and thrive. He left primary school working at age-related expectations for writing.

 REFLECTIVE ACTIVITY

'You imagine that teachers put in place all the things they say they will. Noah was spiralling but it's so hard sometimes to get to the bottom of why when you're not in the school yourself to see. The lack of empathy around the homework was the tipping point. We were fortunate that the head listened and acted. Noah was fortunate he then had the most wonderful teacher for the next two years. Things could have turned out very differently otherwise.'

How can schools listen to caregivers to support the stability of a placement? What is more important – stability or homework?

Chapter summary

- Having a background in education and SEND is probably a protective factor for caregivers communicating effectively with a school. You can be at the mercy of systems that are not child-centred, as well as budgets and waiting lists. But when caregivers are listened to and included, the impact is huge.
- Caregivers are often the experts on their child's SEN and what works because, unlike the class teacher, the parent is the constant factor throughout their child's education. If that constant influence is at capacity, if pressure is put on the household, you may find you have a child coming into school already dysregulated, with a parent who cannot regulate their child because of the pressure.
- It is incredibly hard to advocate for your child when feeling guilt and shame.
- If schools reduce the pressure and build connections with home through listening, kindness and humanity, there will be a capacity to learn.

5 | Co-producing SMART targets in the early years
Faye Waterhouse

This chapter focuses on the co-production of SMART targets with children aged 0–5 years with SEND. In the early years, we can hear the child's voice; gather views, thoughts and feelings; and hear what matters to them. This chapter aims to set out various strategies for children at different stages depending on their cognitive development, also known as their developmental level. A range of approaches to listen to and hear children are shared utilising the early years environment.

Creating the mindset

In the early years, co-producing SMART targets with children can often be daunting because capturing the voice of a child who has additional needs can be difficult, depending on their strengths, interests and challenges. Often, very young children who have complex needs or speech, language and communication difficulties have not had their voices heard in developing their targets. The causal factors contributing to their challenges are varied and can include the inability to communicate verbally due to lack of vocabulary, lack of understanding of questions asked or inability to give attention to a question or task. Furthermore, early years practitioners will have differing training and varying experience working with and listening to children.

Involving children in matters that affect them

It is a positive experience to involve a child in meetings with professionals and caregivers. It should not be assumed that children cannot or should not attend meetings because of their age. You will need to consider how long they attend and the environment you hold any meetings in. Provide resources that interest them and a setting they are familiar with. Creating a child-centred environment makes you more likely to support them in discussions about their education and care. Suppose a child has limited listening skills or is likely to show dysregulated behaviours due to feeling unsettled in this environment, for example, screaming continuously. In that case, alternative methods can be used, such as sharing photographs or videos, or visiting the child in their classroom or a space they feel safe. Sharing videos of the child in the setting is a valuable way of communicating with caregivers and other stakeholders about the child's strengths, interests, needs and struggles in their classroom environment. It can also be used as a tool to show progress towards achieving targets.

The language used in the meeting needs to be age-appropriate. If the child takes part in the meeting, they need to be supported to understand what is being discussed by translating it into child-friendly terms.

Familiar adults

For children in the early years, it is crucial that they work with adults familiar to them and that these adults support the child to capture their voice. Creating positive relationships with children requires trust from both the children and their families. To achieve this, you need to strive for positive interactions with the children through being consistent and reliable so they know routines, boundaries and expectations. Through day-to-day interactions with early years practitioners, they will know what the children like to play with and what stimulates their interest. As connections and relationships develop, adults involved in the education and care of the children will know how best to support their emotional development. Those with whom the child has formed attachments are well placed to support them in voicing their needs, wants and interests, both verbally and non-verbally, to inform the target setting. Intensive interaction strategies used in play promote positive relationships by focusing on the foundations of early interactions: being attentive, showing interest, anticipating, sharing, turn-taking, trusting and respecting. This practical approach by Hewett (2018) can be beneficial in building up a relationship leading to a greater awareness of what matters most to the child/young person.

The environment

Providing an engaging, stimulating and interesting environment in an early years setting is crucial. Children can engage, be stimulated, develop interests and feel safe to have a voice within the early years environment. It is important to remember that children in their early years may develop a voice verbally or non-verbally, depending on their level of need. Settings must enable children to build their vocabulary, ensuring activities are open-ended to promote discussion. Practitioners can ask open-ended questions and enhance with further resources based on conversations with children, as well as displays, lettering and numerals that are at child height.

Communication and language

Communication and language are central to the new EYFS Framework (DfE, 2021). An environment with engaging and interesting open-ended resources can foster language acquisition and the development of vocabulary. For example, activities should ideally not have a right or wrong answer; they should allow for creativity and freedom to explore while developing problem-solving skills. It is the role of the adult to facilitate this and support through provocation and engagements that create a sense of wonder for the children to develop thinking and demonstrate their knowledge and understanding. Stimulation allows the children to develop a voice that they feel confident to share with others and helps them make sense of the world around them. Environments that encapsulate this, along with developing independence and curiosity, support the needs of all children in the classroom.

The suggested strategies later can be used depending on a child's level of cognitive development to ensure they are age- and stage-appropriate, and considerate of their multifaceted needs.

Using puppets

Most children love to engage with puppets, and a child who may have difficulty with face-to-face conversations with an adult may benefit from their use (Figure 5.1). A child could follow the puppet's instructions or begin a conversation, or just feel more comfortable with the puppet's presence. This can be a useful yet simple strategy to give the children a creative communication tool.

Figure 5.1 Puppet

The power of images

Images are a powerful tool to support children with additional needs. They can be in the form of photographs, drawings or symbols. Figure 5.2 shares a drawing by Brin, who wouldn't eat alongside other children in nursery. Brin would wander around the nursery avoiding contact with adults at snack and lunchtime. His key worker had tried different ways to find out why he was reluctant to eat. In the art area, Brin painted the and told his key worker, 'Not on my plate. I don't like peas. I don't like green'.

Other approaches to capturing voice include the following:

* Talk to children about their views, wishes and thoughts
* Photograph or draw their favourite activities
* Take an adult to their favourite places within the school
* Use play dough, construction, art materials and cookery to stimulate conversations
* Give children time to think about and share their ideas

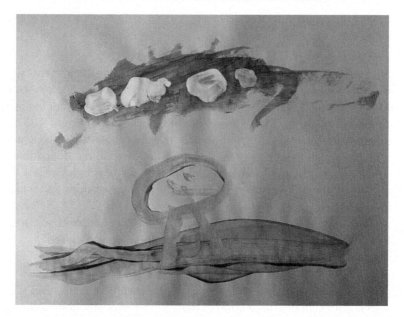

Figure 5.2 Brin's voice through painting

Figure 5.3 What Wilma enjoys doing at nursery

Creative strategies support children to be able to share their views with others. Children may be able to comment on the pictures, photographs or symbols that the adult working with the child can annotate by adding texts or speech bubbles. A further example of this is shown later (Figure 5.3). The drawing was by a 4-year-old child, Wilma. It demonstrates their enjoyment of painting, which this child spends most of her time doing. It also shows the child's voice through comments on her family and her love for her mam, demonstrating her understanding of family relationships and who is important to her.

If children enjoy drawing activities, they may feel relaxed and more able to talk when doing this activity. There are also more structured drawing techniques that can be used to gather views:

- Draw yourself: allows a child to explore their view of themselves
- Draw your school: asks a child to draw their views of school, followed by their ideal school

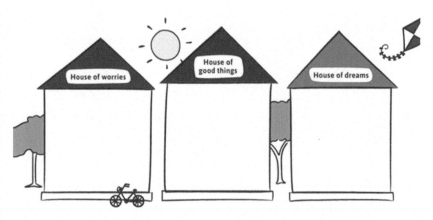

Figure 5.4 Three houses

This allows for discussions about what things might make their current placement better for them.

Another strategy can be using Weld's 'three houses' (2008). For this, an adult would draw three houses named as follows: house of happiness, house of worries and house of dreams (Figure 5.4). Within each house, the child will draw something that makes them happy or worried, or what they dream about. This can enable children to make representations to show insight into their thinking. This can support the formulation of SEN support targets.

This resource has been adapted by 'Me first', from the original Three Houses tool developed in New Zealand by Nicki Weld. Following is an example of an adapted model (Figure 5.5) to relate to schools, to capture the child's voice:

The example in Figure 5.5 was completed by a 5-year-old child with severe learning difficulties. The child was working below their peers in all areas of the early years curriculum. Here, the model demonstrates that the child likes building with blocks, riding bikes and being happy. They are worried about books and state, 'I no read', indicating they are aware that they need to read like their peers but are struggling with this skill. They are also worried about lunchtimes in school. This would be further explored to establish if it is the food they are unhappy with, possibly a

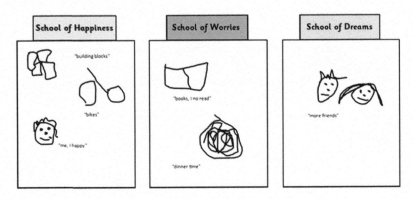

Figure 5.5 Child voice: happiness, worries and dreams

noisy dining hall, the transition into lunchtimes or something else. Their dream school would have more friends. This supports target setting to support making relationships with others and minimising the factors in school that are causing worry or stress to the child, such as reading and lunchtimes. We can use good things to support this; for example, putting letters on the blocks the child likes to play with to reinforce letter recognition.

Case study: Chloe

Chloe was in reception class when she was taken into the care system following the police attending reports of domestic abuse in the family home. She was designated SEN support for her anxieties at school, which presented as nail-biting, hair pulling and rocking. As part of her SEN support review, the teacher asked, 'How can we help you at school'. Chloe asked to draw what she was thinking (Figure 5.6). The teacher said, 'Can you tell me about your picture?' Chloe responded, 'I don't want to come to school. I want to look at the stars with my mam and sister'. The picture was shared with her social worker to explore how her wishes could be granted during contact with her family.

Figure 5.6 Chloe's wishes

Picture exchange communication system (PECS)

This communication tool allows the practitioner and child to communicate when the child has speech, language or communication difficulties. PECS consists of six phases and begins by teaching an individual to give a single picture of a desired item or action to a 'communicative partner', who immediately honours the exchange as a request (Figure 5.7). The system teaches discrimination of pictures and how to put them together in sentences. In the more advanced phases, individuals are taught to use modifiers, answer questions and comment (Pyramid Educational Consultants, 2021).

The child and adult will have a board of images between them, and the child can identify pictures that represent the answer to a question. The images that can be used are very versatile. They could be those from a visual timetable, symbols, real-life photos of the setting, family members or emotions.

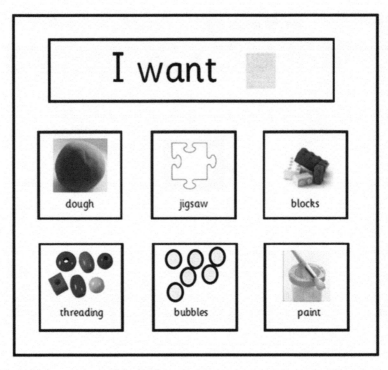

Figure 5.7 Responsive requesting through PECS

PECS were used to support a child aged 5 in reception class with a diagnosis of autism. The child was non-verbal but can demonstrate understanding of simple questions. This tool was used to support the child to make choices throughout the day, support transition times between activities and answer questions.

Audio and video recordings

An audio recording or video clips are the most obvious ways of capturing what's being said, demonstrated or signed. If a child is already using technology to support their communication, consider using the familiar method at a meeting (e.g., recording their voice on a voice output device to play).

Videos of the child in the early years environment can be shared with professionals to support target writing. A conversation example of this would be as follows:

Context: Teacher, SENCO and child (aged 5) watching a five-minute video of the child playing in the construction blocks area within a reception classroom. The child has a diagnosis of autism and has limited communication skills.

Teacher: I think you are enjoying this activity because I can see you are smiling and laughing – is that right?

Child: I like.

SENCO: You like the blocks. You like to build with the blocks.

Teacher: I can see your friend is trying to play with you.

Child: Sam.

SENCO: That's right, it is Sam. He is building a tower with you. Oh dear, you knocked down Sam's tower. Tower all gone.

Child: Sam, no tower.

Teacher: I can see you are building your own tower now. I wonder how tall you can make it. I wonder if Sam will help you.

Child: No, Sam, me do.

This script shows that the child likes to play with the blocks, as the child agrees, 'I like'. The child recognises the other child, Sam's presence. The child is becoming tolerant of other children playing within their space. However, when they feel less able to, the child can destroy the other child's work (i.e., the tower). A target would be set from this to support the child to allow other children into an area where they are playing and play alongside others, slowly incorporating the other children into their play at a later stage.

The Leuven Scale by Laevers (1994)

The Leuven Scale has been developed by a team based at the Research Centre for Experiential Education (Leuven University, Belgium) under Dr Ferre Laevers. Laevers's (1994) tool focuses on two central indicators: wellbeing and involvement. Wellbeing is linked to self-confidence, a reasonable degree of self-esteem and resilience. Involvement refers to being intensely engaged in activities and is considered necessary for deep-level learning and development.

Assessment of wellbeing and involvement

Laevers created a five-point scale to measure both wellbeing and involvement. If there is a lack of wellbeing and/or involvement, a child's development will likely be threatened. The higher the levels of wellbeing and participation we can achieve for the child, the more we can add to the child's development. When there are high levels of wellbeing and involvement, we know that deep-level learning occurs. The evaluation starts with assessing the levels of wellbeing and involvement. It is recommended that practitioners observe the children for about two minutes to ascertain the general levels of wellbeing and involvement using the five-point scale. The observation can focus on groups of children or can be used to focus on a particular individual. Learning will be limited unless a child operates at a higher level on the scale, demonstrating a good level of wellbeing and involvement. However, children cannot peak at these levels all the time, and levels will fluctuate throughout the day. This helps inform us how the child is feeling and how engaged children are with their learning and the environment, supporting capturing the child's voice.

Developing emotions resources

An emotions chart can be used for CYP to identify where they are on a feelings scale. Producing an emotions chart can be done with individual children or in a group to highlight that we all may feel differently. Quite often, this can be completed as part of self-registration in the early years (Figure 5.8). Children find their lollypop stick name and place it in the pocket of the emotion. These can be moved around throughout the day, and the teacher can monitor children's feelings. This helps form a child's voice, as the teacher can understand if there are specific tasks, times of day or activities that the child is more or less happy to be part of.

This self-registration system allows practitioners to see how the children feel when coming into school and at various points throughout the day.

Figure 5.8 Example of an emotional check-in

Questions may be asked to gather views on why a child placed their feeling where they did and what might make them move up or down the ladder. Over time, we may see patterns in emotional changes. For example, a child may feel sad during particular lessons. Monitoring the self-registration supports the identification of how children feel. For example, a child may often place their name on a happy face during maths and a sad face during literacy lessons. This information could be discussed with the child if they can communicate why. Feels ladders take many forms. They can be used with pictures of children showing various emotions, with cartoon face

115

images, or even through colours. This can be developed over time, with the children moving from real-life images to colours as the children mature throughout the school.

Emotional check-ins

Emotional check-ins can be used throughout the day to allow children to share how they are feeling at that time. Generally, they tend to be supported by visuals (emojis, characters, smiley faces or symbols) displaying different feelings (Figure 5.9). However, this could be done verbally if a child fully understands the range of emotions and can discuss them.

Emotional check-ins can be used as an opportunity to explore CYP's understanding of different feelings and to explore which strategies might help support them (e.g., if they are feeling sad or angry, what might make them feel better?).

Happy   Sad

Angry   Confused

Figure 5.9 Emotional symbols

Traffic lights

Traffic lights can be used as a scale to gather views about various topics (green – positive, amber – neutral, red – negative) (Figure 5.10). This

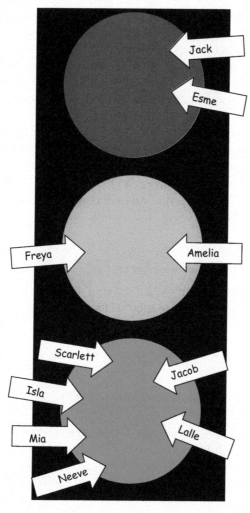

Figure 5.10 Traffic light system to capture child voice

technique can be beneficial for a child to self-reflect on how they have found a task and what their feelings are about things. This can be drawn on work tasks for the child to colour the relevant light afterwards, or it can be completed as a separate activity. The subsequent figure shows a traffic light system for a group of nursery children. Children can place their names on the light colour to demonstrate how they are feeling. For example, the teacher may ask if children understand the task they will be doing next. If they respond with red, this means they do not know what to do; amber, they might need some help; and green, they are ready to go. It is important to remember that younger children may require images of themselves instead of names.

It is also important to gather what helps the children with future development and consider caregiver and child views on what they find difficult. Following children's interests is also paramount in the early years. Activities that are of no interest to the children or have no motivational factor may have a negligible impact on learning and development and achieving targets. This does not necessarily mean that children will be motivated by each activity, but knowing a motivational purpose can enable children to be successful learners.

 REFLECTIVE ACTIVITY

Think of the activities provided in your early years setting. Who has planned them? How are they related to the children's interests, needs and abilities? How do they develop the child further to make progress?

SMART targets in the early years

Following (Table 5.1) is a selection of questions to consider when writing SMART targets for children in the early years and an example of how this would look in practice. Practitioners need to consider each of these questions when determining what is appropriate for each child.

Table 5.1 Developing SMART targets

Non-SMART targets	
Not SMART targets	**Not effective actions**
To stop running off and hitting others	Tell Simon to stop and what it is we want him to do
SMART targets	
Specific**, measurable, achievable, relevant and time-bound**	
Specific SMART targets	*Effective actions*
To understand the stop signal to prevent disruptive behaviours in school (e.g., hitting and throwing objects) Simon will understand the verbal and visual stop signals, and will be observed by staff responding to them to inhibit particular behaviours	Complete stop and go games with Mrs Smith twice per week at an age-appropriate level to encourage Simon's understanding by January 2020, reviewing stop resources throughout Staff to say 'stop' in a firm voice and show the stop picture card when we want Simon to change his behaviour Follow up with what we would like Simon to do and praise his efforts

Chapter summary

- There is value and purpose in capturing a child's voice in early years to see how they view themselves and their learning.
- Caregivers know their child best. Positive relationships with caregivers ensure their views, wishes and thoughts form part of day-to-day practice and provision.
- Listening to children provides an essential insight into the child's mind, allowing us to develop and nurture their thoughts and feelings, and encourage them to reach their full potential.
- A range of systems and processes can be implemented to capture a young child's views and emotions.

Recommended reading

Bee, H. (1989) *The developing child*. New York: Harper & Row.

Davis, P. and Florian, L. (2004) *Teaching strategies and approaches for pupils with special educational needs: A scoping study*. London: Department of Education and Skills.

Department for Education (2021) *Development matters*. Available at: https://assets.publishing.service.gov.uk/government/uploads/system/uploads/attachment_data/file/1007446/6.7534_DfE_Development_Matters_Report_and_illustrations_web__2_.pdf (Accessed: 12 October 2021).

Department for Education and Skills (2001) *Inclusive schooling children with special educational needs*. Nottingham: DfES Publications.

Dunlop, A.W. (2003) 'Bridging children's early education transitions through parental agency and inclusion', *Education in the North*, pp. 55–65.

Greig, A. (2001) *Social understanding goes to school. Supporting the personal, social and emotional competencies of children in transition from nursery to school*. Glasgow: University of Strathclyde.

Hewett, D. (2018) *The intensive interaction handbook*. London: SAGE Publications, Ltd.

Laevers, F. (1994) *The Leuven involvement scale for young children*. Edinburgh: Centre for Experiential Education.

Laevers, F. (2000) 'Forward to basics! Deep-level learning and the experiential approach', *Early Years*, 20(2), pp. 20–29.

Laevers, F. (2003) 'Experiential Education: Making care and education more effective through wellbeing and involvement', in *Involvement of children and teacher style: Insights from an international study on experiential education*, edited by Ferre Laevers and Ludo Heylen, 13–24. Studia Pedagogica 35. Leuven: Leuven University Press.

Laevers, F. (ed.) (2005) *Wellbeing and involvement in care settings: A process-orientated self-evaluation instrument for care settings*. Leuven: Kind & Gezin.

Martin-Denham, S. and Watts, S. (2019) *The SENCO handbook: Leading provision and practice*. London: SAGE Publications, Ltd.

McLean, A. (2003) *The motivating school*. London: Paul Chapman Publishing.

Pyramid Educational Consultants (2021) *What is PECS?* Available at: https://pecs-unitedkingdom.com/pecs/ (Accessed: 5 December 2021).

Sheridan, M., Sharma, A. and Cockerill, H. (2008) *From birth to five years*. London: Routledge.

Sylva, K., Siraj-Blatchford, I. and Taggart, B. (2003) *Assessing quality in the early years. Early childhood environment rating scale*. Extension (ECERS-E) Four Curricular Subscales. Stoke-on-Trent: Trentham Books Ltd.

Weld, N. (2008) *The three houses tool: Building safety and positive change*. Dorset: Russell House Publishing Ltd.

References

Department for Education (DfE) (2021) *Development matters*. Available at: https://assets.publishing.service.gov.uk/government/uploads/system/uploads/attachment_data/file/1007446/6.7534_DfE_Development_Matters_Report_and_illustrations_web__2_.pdf (Accessed: 12 October 2021).

Hewett, D. (2018) *The intensive interaction handbook*. London. SAGE Publications, Ltd.

Laevers, F. (1994) *The Leuven involvement scale for young children (LIS-YC)*. Leuven, Belgium: EXE Project.

Me First (2019) *Me first three houses tool*. Available at: https://www.mefirst.org.uk/resource/me-first-three-houses-tool/ (Accessed: 2 December 2021).

Weld, N. (2008) *The three houses tool: Building safety and positive change*. Dorset: Russell House Publishing Ltd.

6 | Co-production through mindfulness
Donna Walker

This chapter shares The Link School's (a Pupil Referral Unit) mindfulness journey to support CYP in developing strategies to support their emotional regulation. It describes listening to their views to identify their care needs and to support them in developing an awareness of self.

Creating a vision

The Link School works with CYP aged 4–16 and their families across the City of Sunderland. We are proud of our focus on emotional wellbeing, ensuring it is an integral part of the school ethos for our CYP, caregivers and staff. Our REACH vision permeates every aspect of our whole-school life (Figure 6.1). We endeavour to support our school community to be 'Happy and Healthy', where everyone experiences success. We want our CYP to succeed academically, be fully prepared for working life and be active and responsible citizens.

We aim for the following:

- Provide a nurturing and creative environment in which our CYP can flourish and grow to their full potential so they can aspire and achieve.
- Develop a culture where our CYP are recognised as unique individuals and experience a sense of belonging.
- Create an environment that effectively breaks down the barriers to learning, enabling our CYP to achieve individual excellence.
- Promote emotional wellbeing and resilience in our CYP, who are then able to regulate emotions to live safe, healthy and fulfilling lives.

DOI: 10.4324/9781003261506-7

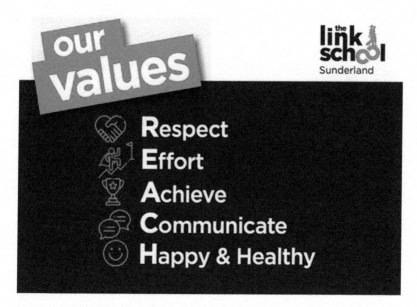

Figure 6.1 The Link School values

- Raise aspirations so our CYP and their families have the confidence and skills to prepare for their next life stage.

The CYP at our school has a variety of SEMH needs, as described in the SEND code of practice (DfE and DoH, 2015, p. 98):

> Children and young people may experience a wide range of social and emotional difficulties which manifest themselves in many ways. These may include becoming withdrawn or isolated, as well as displaying challenging, disruptive or disturbing behaviour. These behaviours may reflect underlying mental health difficulties such as anxiety or depression, self-harming, substance misuse, eating disorders or physical symptoms that are medically unexplained. Other children and young people may have disorders such as attention deficit disorder, attention deficit hyperactive disorder or attachment disorder.

The term *SEMH* emphasises that behaviours are often ways of communicating something more significant or underlying. This recognition of behaviour as a form of communication is a critical element that underpins our mindful practice and permeates our whole-school curriculum intent.

Curriculum intent

Curriculum intent can be exhibited in many ways depending on a school's context and improvement journey. Still, it is essential to keep a focus on the Ofsted School Inspection Handbook, which outlines the vision and ambition for the curriculum. Curriculum intent is 'The extent to which the school's curriculum sets out the knowledge and skills that pupils will gain at each stage' (Ofsted, 2021, s. 195). Ofsted will also consider how the curriculum developed or adopted by the school is taught and assessed to support CYP in building their knowledge and applying it as skills (we call this 'implementation'). Finally, inspectors will consider their outcomes due to their education (we call this the 'impact'). There is a recognition throughout the Ofsted Framework (2021) that schools have the flexibility to take different approaches to their curriculum design. We have thought carefully about this while embarking on our mindful journey.

Beginning a mindful journey

I'm never a believer in luck, more a believer in fate. Three years ago, fate brought Nicole to The Link School. Nicole, The Magic Fairy, is infectious. She is kind and compassionate. She brings love into her work; the world and children and people around her know and write about this (Figure 6.2). Nicole has expertise in a range of wellbeing techniques, including reiki, Indian head massage, meditation and mindfulness.

One of the most well-recognised definitions of *mindfulness* is by Dr Jon Kabat-Zinn. He defined *mindfulness* as 'paying attention in a particular way: on purpose, in the present moment, and non-judgmentally' (Black, 2011, p. 28). Nicole advocates mindfulness as a way of keeping a moment-by-moment awareness of thoughts, feelings, bodily sensations and the surrounding environment through a gentle, nurturing perspective. Through

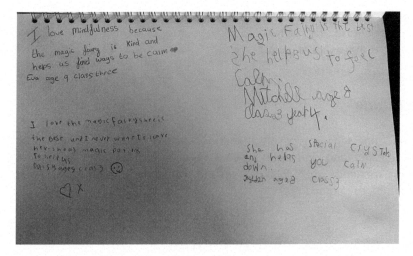

Figure 6.2 The children's views on the Magic Fairy

mindfulness, thoughts tune into our senses, being in the moment rather than thinking about the past or imagining the future.

Three basic components of mindfulness are intention, attention and attitude.

Intention

The intention is what you hope to achieve from practising mindfulness. You may want to relieve stress, gain emotional balance or discover your true self. The strength of your intention helps to motivate you to practise mindfulness and shapes the quality of your mindful awareness, and it is important to pinpoint what that is.

Attention

Mindfulness is about paying attention to your inner or outer experience in the present moment. Your mindful attention is mainly developed through various types of meditation, from observing an object to participating in a group exercise. The key is not to allow your focus to drift from what you are doing at that exact moment.

Attitude

Mindfulness involves paying attention to certain attitudes, such as curiosity, acceptance and kindness. Our CYP are encouraged to start their journey and experience where it takes them and share their learning and accept the differences in others.

Developing a mindful culture

Creating a mindful culture is not something that happens overnight. It's about taking a leap of faith and having the passion for developing a school culture that is supportive, open and free from negativity to be genuinely happy and healthy. Our school has gone beyond committing to mindfulness; it embraces a devotion to a whole-school wellbeing culture, promoting good mental, physical and emotional wellbeing. Everyone must be appreciated and valued equally, a leadership vision that the entire school embraces. Wellbeing 'is for everyone; it is for every day. It needs to be applied equally and it needs to be nurtured and authentic. Wellbeing will develop where the culture of the school enables it to succeed' (Cowley, 2019, p. 61).

It is important to recognise mindfulness as an integral part of the curriculum. It is built directly into all school timetables and links into other subjects in the curriculum. 'Adding a mindfulness framework around your existing subject matter and pedagogical expertise will serve to increase academic, social and emotional learning' (Mussey, 2021, p. 25). Mindfulness is embedded across the curriculum (Table 6.1). Figure 6.3 shares how seasonal customs can be used as a basis for CYP to reflect on and share their experiences.

Mindfulness is practised in many ways at The Link School, often determined by the CYP. All CYP sessions include a mindfulness starter – bubble

Table 6.1 Mindfulness planning linked to the seven core attitudes of creative mindfulness

Duration: Seven weeks (one lesson per class per week) One-to-one interventi on when needed	Cross-curricular links: Life skills, art, PSHEE and Spanish
Relevance	Understanding mindfulness
Cross-curricular links	Life skills, art, PSHEE and Spanish
Other useful resources	Pinterest Nursing school's art therapy Anna Freud Mental health awareness calendar Contended child mental health resources MIND NHS BBC Sounds – Relax Apple podcasts – meditation/relaxation ASMR
The seven core attitudes of creative mindfulness	
Stop, breathe, create	Learn to have a still, calm mind; take a breath; go slow; and be patient with oneself and practice
Patience/kindness	Go easy and gentle with yourself – more self-compassion
Curiosity	Discover new things: What is this sensation? What is this thought? How am I feeling right now?
Persistence	Keep on showing up; keep on being curious; when feeling tired, grumpy or sad, show up – as this is the time you will need mindfulness the most
Allowing	Take one moment at a time; allow feelings and thoughts, as allowing is an act of kindness to oneself
Trusting	Whatever happens, trust it; there is no right or wrong way; trust yourself
Playfulness	Don't take yourself or things too seriously; play comes naturally; allow time to explore and play

blowing to control breathing; essential oils, such as lavender or citrus oil; candles to enrich the senses; and calming parachute work to promote team-work. The CYP are then encouraged to take time out to discuss thoughts

Figure 6.3 Mindfulness across the curriculum

and feelings in a calm and supportive environment before spending time engaging in focused creative work.

Meditation is a practice for calming the mind and body. It can be as simple as listening to music or relaxing to a visualised script. There is a no-pressure rule here, as every CYP is different and will arrive at their meditation journey at their own pace. Meditation spaces are vital to give time and space to every student (Figures 6.4 and 6.5), and celebrate our commitment to this journey.

Figure 6.4 Meditation space

Figure 6.5 The mindful journey

Mindful communication allows us to hear and listen to ourselves. It provides us with a chance to adjust our thoughts and feelings, and use non-verbal cues with kindness, compassion and attention within a non-judgemental environment. An example shown in Figure 6.6 shares a Link School collaborative and collective piece in response to a CYP feeling after visiting the knife angel (national monument against violence and aggression). It helped them share how they feel about the negative effects of violent behaviour.

Figure 6.6 Collaborative reflection

Mindful bracelets and decorations (Figure 6.7 and Figure 6.8) were made by CYP to support the Young Minds #HelloYellow campaign, which raised awareness of mental health issues in CYP. The CYP have become more aware of their emotions, social and family interactions, positive problem-solving, growth mindset, and overall wellbeing.

Figure 6.7 Mindful bracelet

Figure 6.8 Raising awareness of mental health

The shared learning of our CYP

Throughout their time in school, it is vital that our CYP feel their voice is heard and that they own the mindful work they do. A mindful journal is a

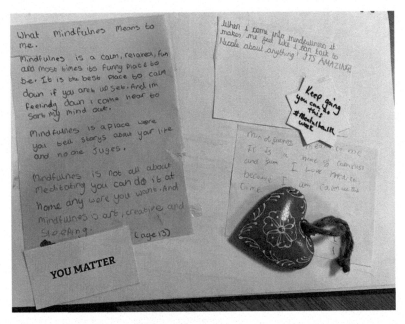

Figure 6.9 Extracts from a mindful journal

place where their journey and voice are shared. Figure 6.9 shares extracts of journal entries from some of our key stage 3 CYP.

Outdoor mindfulness

We launched Edible Playground with Trees for Cities (a UK charity working on a national and international scale to improve lives by planting trees in cities) during the COVID-19 pandemic. Our Edible Playground offered a sensory area alongside a food-growing area across the site. The development of the Edible Playground played a crucial role in supporting children with their behaviour management and meeting their sensory needs. A vital feature was to incorporate food growing, preparing, cooking and eating throughout the school and encourage healthy eating. We embedded the initiative into the school curriculum to become an integrated outdoor learning resource across all curriculum areas.

Figure 6.10 and *Figure 6.11* Edible Playgrounds

COVID-19 and school closures have impacted what we wanted to create with our edible gardens in the first year. However, we used this to our advantage and worked with our CYP to harvest their first crops. The CYP planted beetroot, carrots, tomatoes, strawberries, potatoes and a variety of flowers, including lavender, which the pupils used in emotional wellbeing packs that they made for each other and staff.

The benefits of our Edible Playground on mindfulness

Our children do their best when calm, relaxed and well supported. We thrive on our relationships with our CYP, particularly during our edible garden and mindfulness sessions. We created a calming environment and ensured that everyone felt included, supported and listened to. Our learners initially felt very sceptical that breathing exercises, thoughtful activities and relaxation techniques would work for them but now remind each other of the positive benefits during times of high anxiety or stress, especially in an outdoor environment where they can grow. This was reinforced by taking part in our gardening activities, where they were able to take the time to learn new skills by growing produce and then cooking with it.

Through our collaboration with Edible Playgrounds, we have created an outdoor element environment where all our children can express themselves and learn how to support their mental health by improving their understanding of healthy eating options. The inclusion of outdoor mindfulness into the school curriculum positively impacted the emotional wellbeing of both staff and CYP. Creative mindfulness and how it is delivered within the school encourage our young people to deal with their thoughts and feelings outside the classroom. The impact on pupil behaviour and engagement has been remarkable, resulting in fewer crisis incidents within the setting and a more considered approach to their behaviour.

Upon completing the Edible Playgrounds project, Nicole and the Edible Playground leads incorporated mindfulness into our outdoor spaces (Figure 6.12 and Figure 6.13). Outdoor meditations sessions gave CYP time to connect with the world around them. Soft furnishings are a simple way to support CYP in sensory meditation.

Figure 6.12 and *Figure 6.13* Outdoor meditation

At the Link School, we promote self-care. Figures 6.12 and 6.13 share photographs of our young people connecting with the outdoors. Mindful breathing is a fundamental and powerful mindfulness practice (Figure 6.14). The idea is to focus the attention on your breathing, its natural rhythm and flow, and how it feels on each inhale and exhale. Through this experience, they are afforded time to breathe and be present with themselves and each other (Figure 6.15).

Figure 6.14 Mindful breathing techniques to connect to the natural world

Figure 6.15 Time to breathe and be present

Case study 1: Lee

Lee was permanently excluded from his mainstream school when he was 13. He has SEMH needs and has exhibited challenging and aggressive behaviour. Through the mindfulness sessions, Lee began to see that his behaviours were linked to his anxieties. Through self-identifying his worries, he was able to take ownership and begin to accept support.

During the COVID-19 lockdown, Lee's mum rang the school to share her concerns about her son and how he was struggling with a low mood. A meditation session was arranged to relax him enough to share his concerns and what was worrying him in response to the phone call.

On his return to school, Lee was able to speak openly to others about his worries and how he 'was proud of himself for not kicking off'. He was able to talk freely about asking 'for his time to think' and 'time to share' strategies, which helped him improve his behaviour.

Mindful gardening

Mindful meditation takes many forms. We adopted the mindful gardening approach. Mindful gardening is a caring way to garden, connecting with the earth to cultivate a healthy mind, and can be a great form of mindfulness meditation to feel calm and relaxed. Even with limited outdoor space, you can adopt and embed mindful gardening approaches. Figures 6.16 and 6.17 showcase how our outdoor areas have been transformed as part of the mindful gardening approach. Figure 6.18 shows an example of how our older CYP take ownership of their mindful gardens and how they use this time to channel their energies into improving their emotional wellbeing.

Supporting children and families during school holidays

School holidays are when most vulnerable CYP struggle with their emotional wellbeing and often display anxious and challenging behaviours in the home environment. This can lead to instability in the home and impact a CYP's self-esteem and self-image. This is often highlighted more at

139

Figure 6.16 Mindful garden

Figure 6.17 Outdoor spaces to support mindful gardening approaches

Christmastime, with the focus being on a family. Our Mindful Moments pro-gramme was developed to provide a two-day drop-in service at one of our school sites during the Christmas holidays. The purpose was to support CYP who were struggling with their emotional wellbeing and who could come into school and use 'creative mindfulness, meditation and relaxation tech-niques to bring a sense of calm and balance'. We added a touch base phone call session between 9 am and 3 pm on those days to strengthen the offer.

141

Figure 6.18 Preparing the soil for planting

Over the following 12 months, the programme was expanded to all school holidays, with caregivers invited to participate. The impact was a notable improvement in the behaviour of the CYP who engaged in the programme and an increase in the openness in sharing how they have felt in those sessions (Figure 6.19).

Case study 2: Andrew

Andrew started at The Link School following a short placement at a specialist provision. He has a diagnosis of ADHD and attachment disorder. Following the transition from primary education to mainstream secondary school at the start of year 7, it was identified that he was struggling to manage his emotions. His caregivers agreed it would be in his best interests to

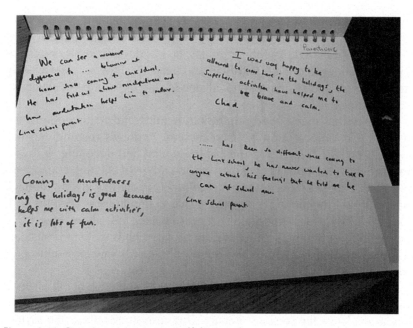

Figure 6.19 Caregiver voice in a mindful journal

transition him to The Link School. Andrew initially had difficulty building relationships with staff and peers and preferred to isolate himself away from the class. As he settled into class and the structured routines, he demonstrated a good sense of humour and a desire to do well in lessons.

While at The Link School, Andrew has made progress through a highly differentiated curriculum, allowing him to complete tasks independently and experience some success. However, he still required a high level of support from staff due to his difficulties processing and retaining information. Andrew's caregivers have been an integral part of his SEN support plan, with regular reviews and meetings, particularly in the early days and weeks.

Andrew has benefitted from working in a smaller class with high support levels. He requires individual support to explain new ideas and have instructions broken down into small steps. Andrew found it challenging to remain on task for parts of each lesson and was easily distracted. He initially struggled to verbalise his feelings and was often involved in conflicts with his peers because he could not see things from somebody else's point of view. Andrew can now accept advice from staff and has put strategies in place himself to remain calm. With focused support and regular PSHEE and structured play opportunities, he has developed his emotional skills and reduced conflicts with staff and peers. Andrew accesses weekly mindfulness sessions and additional one-to-one appointments when he requests them.

Andrew has made good progress in reading and writing due to the Reading Plus Intervention he is accessing. Andrew's reading age has gone up to 16.2 from 12.3, and his inferential and decoding skills are now the best in class. He also uses a wide range of exciting vocabulary to enhance the effectiveness of his writing. Nicole has given feedback that Andrew is becoming more responsive to mindfulness sessions and, during weekly group mindfulness sessions, can talk about how he is feeling in front of others. She feels the progress he is making is vast, as, at the start of her work with him, he used to say, 'I have no feelings, or I don't know'.

Andrew now uses coloured Play-Doh to talk and write about his feelings (red for anger and green for calm). This hands-on approach is a positive way to evidence the sessions' impact. This case study reflects the saying, 'it's a village to raise a child'. To be more exact, our CYP must be equipped with the skills to become responsible and active citizens within the context of our setting or any setting. They need to be supported to have positive and meaningful interactions that provide them with skills to survive later in life. Mental health first-aiders in schools are essential, not just for signposting students to support themselves but, more importantly, equipping them with the tools and skills to be resilient learners. The gift of self-sufficiency is the most powerful gift we can give our vulnerable learners through the curriculum and through our mental health first-aiders.

Mindful targets

The review of school exclusion in Sunderland highlighted this:

> During the exclusion, they are often not doing anything purposeful with their time or being supported to understand any underlying reasons for their

behaviour that led to an exclusion. The caregivers struggled to maintain employment or good mental health due to the stress of the uncertainty of their child's future. Children and caregivers need to understand why the exclusion happened and be supported to rebuild relationships within families and re-engage with education.

(Martin-Denham, 2020)

The mindful journey begins with the need to identify and break down these barriers to re-engage a child and their family with a positive school experience; only when they feel safe and secure can teaching really have an impact on their learning.

Assessment is a crucial part of this process. In education, *assessment* refers to 'the wide variety of methods or tools that educators use to evaluate, measure and document the academic readiness, learning progress, skill acquisition or educational needs of students' (The Glossary of Education Reform, 2015). However, emotional dysregulation cannot be easily scaled, making the assessment of improvement more challenging to track and monitor. Therefore, it is essential to completely understand all the CYP's needs by adopting a strengths-based approach. This can 'shift the very purpose of assessment from merely providing information to the 'assessor' (teacher) to sharing positive information with the 'assessed' (learner). Not only does this have the potential to boost their confidence and self-esteem, but it also provides meaningful information about the skills that they have and could attempt to apply to aid future learning' (Carter, 2021).

This is the basis for the comprehensive use of support planning using the four-part cycle (assess, plan, do and review) (DfE and DoH, 2015). Through this cycle, actions are reviewed and refined to understand a CYP's needs, and the support required to help them secure good outcomes increases. This is known as the graduated response.

Mindfulness is an integral part of the curriculum. We felt that mindful targets have a purposeful place in our graduated response, so we built these targets into support plans as part of a child-centred approach (Table 6.2). Nicole works closely with the class teacher and SENCOs to identify mindful targets and devise ways to support them during group and one-to-one mindful sessions.

Table 6.2 A sample of Andrew's targets as part of an SEN support plan

Specific target	Measurable	Achievable	Relevant	Time-bound
To accept that peers hold different views and to respond without becoming angry	Andrew will remain calm during group activities and talk about different opinions without becoming upset	Staffing resource of 2:7 available to support Andrew during group activities	Andrew has stated he wants to have fewer disputes with his peers	By the Christmas holidays 2022
To articulate his emotions and express them appropriately	Andrew will tell staff how he is feeling and ask for support if he is feeling angry	A counsellor working with Andrew to provide one-to-one support, recognising the spectrum of emotions	Andrew gets embarrassed when he has been angry and has asked for help managing his reactions to others	By the Christmas holidays 2022

Review
- Andrew continues to struggle to see other people's viewpoints and does not listen or want to recognise that other people have a different opinion to him. This can be challenging during lessons like PSHEE, where class discussions and debates are encouraged.
- Peers often feel frustrated that Andrew needs to have the last word in conversations, which can escalate to the point where there can be disputes and conflicts in class.
- Andrew is making some progress in sessions with Nicole. He is opening up more about his feelings during weekly mindfulness lessons and accessing her on a one-to-one basis. He is beginning to use creativity to describe how he feels, using things like coloured Play-Doh to represent emotions.
- Andrew still needs to understand that staff offer advice or interventions to keep him on track and to prevent conflict with peers. Because he cannot see things from other people's viewpoints, this remains an ongoing target.

Chapter summary

- Emotional wellbeing and a mindful community should be at the heart of the ethos of the school
- Empowering caregivers to be open to mindfulness approaches comes from connecting home to school through shared experiences

- To promote a mindful culture, children and staff need to have a positive can-do approach
- It is important to recognise staff are the most valuable resources who need to be valued, supported and encouraged to develop professionally and personally

 ## Further reading

Cann, G. (2021) *Mindfulness for beginners: A practical guide to finding peace and happiness in an anxious world.* Norfolk: Chas Cann Company, Ltd.

Cherry, L. (2021) *Conversations that make a difference for children and young people: Relationship-focused practice from the frontline.* London: Routledge.

Guber, T., Kalish, L. and Fatus, S. (2005) *Yoga pretzels: 50 fun yoga activities for kids and grownups.* New York: Abrams Books.

Sanderson, C. (2016) *The mini book of mindfulness: Simple meditation practices to help you live in the moment.* Philadelphia: Running Press Miniature Editions.

References

Black, D.S. (2011) 'A brief definition of mindfulness', *Behavioral Neuroscience*, 7(2), pp. 1–2.

Carter, J. (2021) *SEND assessment: A strengths-based framework for learners with SEND.* London: Routledge.

Cowley, A. (2019) *The wellbeing toolkit sustaining, supporting and enabling school staff.* London: Bloomsbury Education.

Department for Education (DfE) and Department of Health (DoH) (2015) *Special educational needs and disability code of practice: 0 to 25 years.* London: DfE.

Martin-Denham, S. (2020) 'A review of school exclusion on the mental health, well-being of children and young people in the City of Sunderland.' Sunderland: University of Sunderland.

Mussey, S. (2021) *Mindfulness in the classroom: Mindful principles for social and emotional learning.* London: Routledge.

Ofsted (2021) *School inspection handbook.* Available at: https://www.gov.uk/government/publications/school-inspection-handbook-eif/school-inspection-handbook (Accessed: 9 December 2021).

The Glossary of Education Reform (2015) *The Glossary of Education Reform for Journalists, Parents, and Community members. By Great Schools Partnership,(last updated: 08.12. 15).*

7 | Re-engaging children and young people through forest school approach

Donna Walker

'If you go down in the woods today, you're sure of a big surprise' (*The Teddy-Bear's Picnic* lyrics). Imagine this being your first thought of forest school. Well, this was mine; no real understanding of what the children did or why. Through this chapter, I share our forest school journey and our learning discovered through the CYP at the school. Imagine what happens when you go down to the woods and see the trees in Figures 7.1 and 7.2. We experience a sense of inner peace and instant calm wash over us; this is the beginning of the adventure.

The Link School vision

As an AP in Sunderland, The Link School's motto 'REACH' encapsulates the school's core values of respect, effort, achievement, communication and happiness. The school aims to REACH everyone through our inclusive approach, including children, caregivers, staff and the wider community. Our staff strive to give the children high aspirations. Because of their challenges with schooling; they don't have them for themselves. We give children and practitioners a shared understanding of our REACH vision through their forest school experience. This approach enables the children to be independent, self-motivated,

DOI: 10.4324/9781003261506-8

Figure 7.1 and *Figure 7.2* Forest school at Herrington Country Park

courageous and considerate, and sets them up for lifelong learning. Forest school supports self-esteem and self-confidence through first-hand experiences that can still be linked back into their formal learning.

Experiencing your development and learning outdoors is inherently different from 'being' in the outdoors. The moment you step outside and are receptive, you will receive different answers to questions, and increase in your sensory and inner life, all because the whole field of experience is now larger and more complex. You are no longer within four walls but a component within a larger biological and ecological system (Cree and Robb, 2021, p. 7).

Finding love for learning

Our primary curriculum is designed to re-engage children in the enjoyment and fun that forest school can offer them. They explore in an enriched language environment designed using the six principles of nurture groups as its foundation:

- Children's learning is understood developmentally
- The classroom offers a safe base
- Nurture is important for the development of wellbeing and self-esteem
- Language is understood as a vital means of communication
- All behaviour is communication
- Transition is important in children's lives

We provide a personalised offer across the curriculum that is relevant to the needs of the children. The curriculum is inclusive and accessible to every child, and flexible and adaptable to their background and needs. Our creative curriculum has a culture of experiential, interactive, physically engaging and stimulating activities to promote interest, curiosity, exploration and engagement.

For those children entering within our infants' phase, learning is categorised as follows:

- Learning and development
- Communication and language

- Physical development
- Personal, social and emotional

In addition, there are four key areas: literacy, mathematics, understanding of the world and expressive art and design.

Figures 7.3 and 7.4 shows how indoor provision delivers our curriculum ethos, encouraging curiosity, investigation and child-led learning experiences. Throughout the nurture approach, teachers can skilfully link their expert subject knowledge to their assessment of prior learning and understanding. The use of enquiry-led learning supports pupil independence. This can be seen through the investigation station where enquiry skills were linked to magic beans and what makes things grow. This was supported by the exploration of light sources where the children could articulate what light sources were and why they were important.

Figure 7.3 Child-led learning

Figure 7.4 Child-led experiences

Why forest school?

Knight (2016, p. 49) states that 'forest school aims to foster a relationship with nature through regular personal experiences in order to develop long term environmentally, sustainable attitudes and practices in staff, learners and the wider community'. Within our setting, forest school offers all children regular opportunities to achieve and develop confidence and self-esteem through hands-on learning experiences in a local woodland or natural environments with trees and natural resources.

Fundamentally, forest school enables us to extend learning beyond the classroom and provides us with the opportunity to combine traditional education practice with our happy and healthy ethos to adopt a mindful approach to learning and wellbeing. We inherently believe that by giving children the freedom to choose how they approach their work, they become motivated to learn. Figures 7.5 and 7.6 shows children taking part

153

Figure 7.5 and *Figure 7.6* A forest school lesson

in a forest school lesson. The lesson objectives were linked to safely using simple tools, considering and caring for local wildlife during winter, and creating Halloween-themed bird feeders. Figures 7.7 and 7.8 provide samples of writing as children reflected on their experiences of forest school back in the classroom

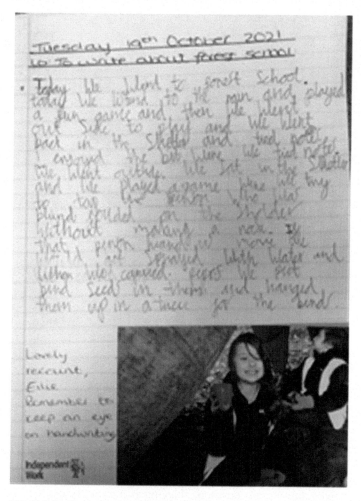

Figure 7.7 Child reflections on outdoor learning

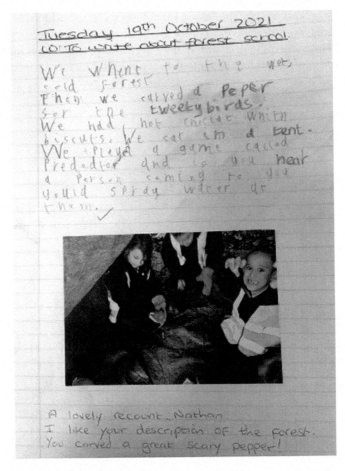

Figure 7.8 Extended writing from forest school experiences

Curriculum planning

Throughout the planning process, it is essential to ensure the national curriculum expectations are covered. 'Playing in nature' is claimed to support creativity, problem-solving, emotional and intellectual development in middle childhood (Kellert, 2005). It is using this premise that the objectives of the forest school curriculum are woven into the short- and long-term planning (Table 7.1) to do the following:

- Develop resilience, confidence, self-esteem and self-help
- Develop skills required to solve problems
- Use an investigative approach and develop scientific skills, such as curiosity, prediction, testing hypothesis and decision-making
- Explore and understand changes in seasons, growth of living things, care of the environment, experiment with state of materials and use of scientific language
- Use and develop senses in an exploratory approach
- Encourage curiosity and a love of nature
- Develop spatial awareness and motor development
- Create a teamwork approach, leadership skills, social awareness and interactions
- Enable children to follow their learning, thinking styles, interests and directions
- Develop personalised, child-led learning, and review and recognise own achievements

Facilitating learning

Forest school leaders see their role as facilitators of child-led learning and, as children gain confidence in forest school settings, help them to negotiate their meaning (Harris, 2017, p. 273). Positive relationships, forest school expertise and knowledge of the children are essential to effective planning and delivery of forest school activities. Without this, there is lack of purpose and understanding. As much as children need a clear structure and boundaries within a framework of self-exploration and discovery, school staff are there to facilitate rather than lead the learning (Figures 7.9 and 7.10). The role of adults in forest school is to support child's exploration, provide information and supervise activities. It is essential that they can do the following:

- See themselves as a child too
- Be as absorbed in an activity as you would expect a child to be
- Build resilience in the children and encourage engagement in activities
- Give feedback to forest school leader and evaluate children's forest experience

Table 7.1 An example of how medium-term planning fit into the overall curriculum

	Autumn 1
Weeks 1 and 2	**Learning objective (LO):** To be comfortable exploring the forest environment To familiarise themselves with nature **Questions:** How do spiders make their webs? What shapes can you see? Why do they make webs? **Theory:** Children to become confident in exploring nature and learn through first-hand experience. Children to focus on creatures of the forest and how they survive. **Practical:** • Complete a scavenger hunt • Find spiderwebs • Investigate spiderwebs and, with materials provided, see if they can make a web strong enough to hold a stone spider or a large web to hold a person
Weeks 3 and 4	**LO:** To use simple knots to make a wind chime **Questions:** What shapes can they make with sticks? How can they tie them together? Which natural materials can they find to make an attractive wind chime? **Theory:** Children to learn simple knot skills and apply them to different situations **Practical:** • Practise simple knot skills (begin with overhand knot) • Look at examples of wind chimes • Investigate forest to find suitable sticks to form a wind chime
Weeks 5 and 6	**LO:** To continue to develop knot skills To use simple tools safely To consider and care for local wildlife during winter. **Questions:** How do you use a knife safely? Can you design a face? What creatures might want to eat the pepper? How do birds find food in winter? **Theory:** Children to follow instructions to use tools safely and responsibly to build confidence and feel a sense of responsibility **Practical:** • Can children remember the overhand knot from last week? • Practise the overhand know and then try the figure-eight knot to use as a stopper knot. • Have adult model safe use of a knife (wearing safety glove and sitting in a safe position away from others). Children cut pepper and scrape out seeds, then design and cut out a Halloween face. Children can leave them in the forest to feed wildlife or fill with birdseed to hang in trees.

Figure 7.9 and *Figure 7.10* Enabling curiosity

The child's experience

Forest school has environmental awareness at the heart of its ethos. Wherever possible, environmentally friendly products and recycled materials are used when appropriate. Good practice is modelled by adults showing children that the world in which we live in should be cared for. Children should feel safe and confident in having a go at new experiences or a repeated experience that they feel comfortable doing. Figures 7.11, 7.12 and 7.13

Figure 7.11 Experiencing the outdoors

Figure 7.12 and *Figure 7.13* Supporting risk-taking behaviours

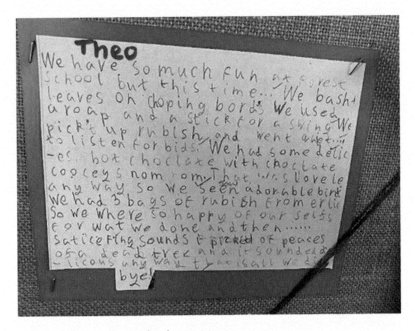

Figure 7.14 Sharing forest school experiences

show how we teach children about careful risk-taking behaviour. For example, completing site checks, participating in team-building activities and sharing new experiences.

Children can take responsibility for choosing appropriate clothing (wearing gloves or a hat in colder weather) and know how to stay safe; for example, knowing if a tree is safe to climb. Part of the forest school experience is promoting the development of core communication and interaction skills that allow them to treat others with respect and value their opinions and their own. As shown in Figure 7.14, you can read the excitement Theo has for forest school: 'we have so much fun at forest school'.

Assessing the impact

To measure the success of forest school, we have carried out weekly assessments of the children, using the Leuven wellbeing and involvement scales

(Figure 7.15 and Figure 7.16). The Leuven scale is a five-point scale that measure a child's emotional wellbeing and involvement. The idea of emotional wellbeing and involvement is particularly important in early years because it safeguards a child's emotional development while encouraging engagement for learning development. It was developed by Leuven University, Belgium, under the supervision of Dr Ferre Laevers.

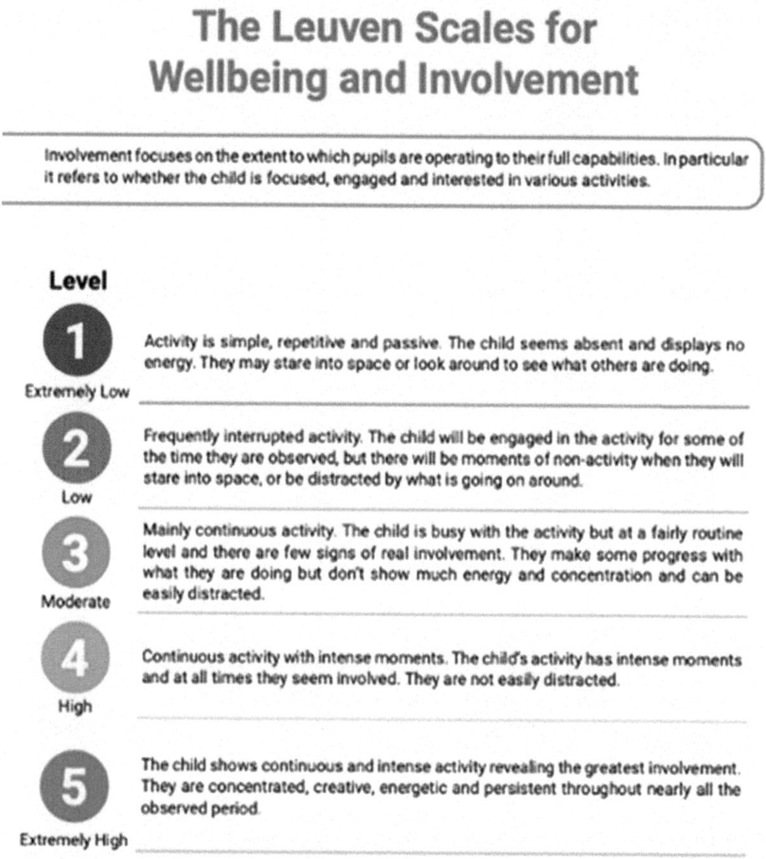

The Leuven Scales for Wellbeing and Involvement

Involvement focuses on the extent to which pupils are operating to their full capabilities. In particular it refers to whether the child is focused, engaged and interested in various activities.

Level

1 Extremely Low — Activity is simple, repetitive and passive. The child seems absent and displays no energy. They may stare into space or look around to see what others are doing.

2 Low — Frequently interrupted activity. The child will be engaged in the activity for some of the time they are observed, but there will be moments of non-activity when they will stare into space, or be distracted by what is going on around.

3 Moderate — Mainly continuous activity. The child is busy with the activity but at a fairly routine level and there are few signs of real involvement. They make some progress with what they are doing but don't show much energy and concentration and can be easily distracted.

4 High — Continuous activity with intense moments. The child's activity has intense moments and at all times they seem involved. They are not easily distracted.

5 Extremely High — The child shows continuous and intense activity revealing the greatest involvement. They are concentrated, creative, energetic and persistent throughout nearly all the observed period.

Figure 7.15 Leuven Scale

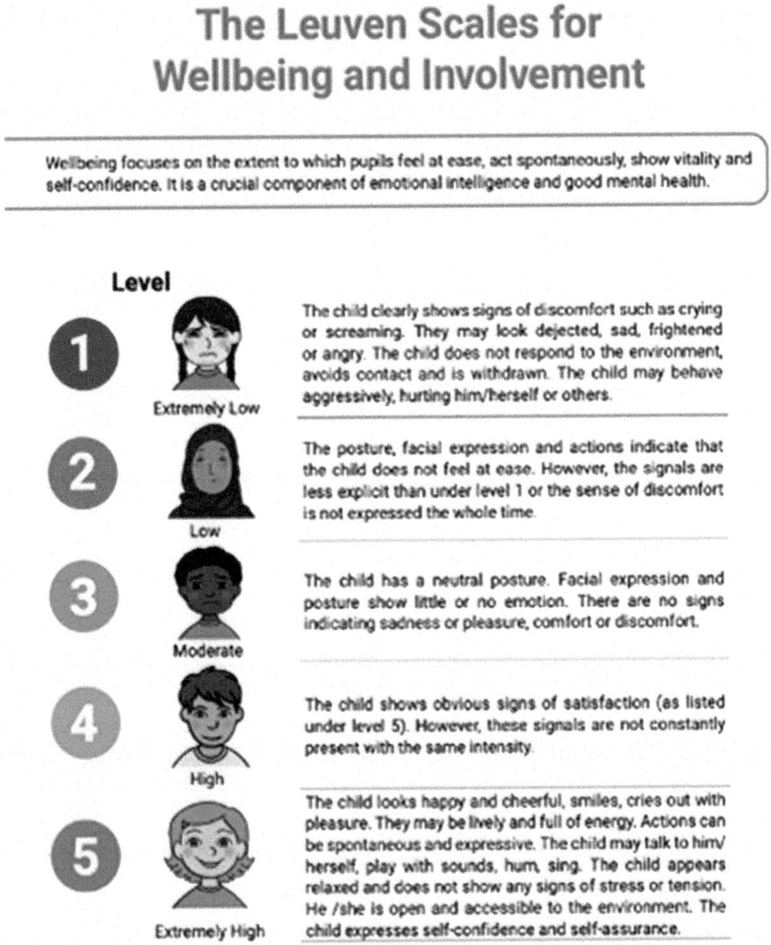

The Leuven Scales for Wellbeing and Involvement

Wellbeing focuses on the extent to which pupils feel at ease, act spontaneously, show vitality and self-confidence. It is a crucial component of emotional intelligence and good mental health.

Level

1 — Extremely Low
The child clearly shows signs of discomfort such as crying or screaming. They may look dejected, sad, frightened or angry. The child does not respond to the environment, avoids contact and is withdrawn. The child may behave aggressively, hurting him/herself or others.

2 — Low
The posture, facial expression and actions indicate that the child does not feel at ease. However, the signals are less explicit than under level 1 or the sense of discomfort is not expressed the whole time.

3 — Moderate
The child has a neutral posture. Facial expression and posture show little or no emotion. There are no signs indicating sadness or pleasure, comfort or discomfort.

4 — High
The child shows obvious signs of satisfaction (as listed under level 5). However, these signals are not constantly present with the same intensity.

5 — Extremely High
The child looks happy and cheerful, smiles, cries out with pleasure. They may be lively and full of energy. Actions can be spontaneous and expressive. The child may talk to him/herself, play with sounds, hum, sing. The child appears relaxed and does not show any signs of stress or tension. He /she is open and accessible to the environment. The child expresses self-confidence and self-assurance.

Figure 7.16 An example of the Leuven Scales for Wellbeing and Involvement, and how these are used to track improvements in pupils' wellbeing
Reference: https://www.twinkl.co.uk/resource/tf-pa-260-the-leuven-scales-observation-resource-pack

Case study

The primary team ran forest school from September 2021 as an ongoing programme continuing throughout the academic year. The children experience the changes in the seasons; develop self-help skills, independence and teamwork; and assess and manage own risks. The programme was accessed by all children who attend the primary phase of The Link School. This cohort consisted of 14 children.

To measure the success of forest school, we carried out weekly assessments using the Leuven wellbeing and involvement scales. The results in Table 7.3 show that 11 out of 14 children exhibited improvements in both the wellbeing and involvement observational criteria.

Table 7.2 Pre- and post-assessment data using the Leuven Scales measure

Child	Wellbeing initial	Involvement initial	Wellbeing final	Involvement final	Wellbeing difference	Involvement difference
1	4.5	4.5	5	5	10%	10%
2	4	3	5	5	20%	40%
3	4.5	4.5	5	5	10%	10%
4	4.5	4.5	5	5	10%	10%
5	4	4	5	5	20%	20%
6	4.5	4.5	5	5	10%	10%
7	4	4.5	5	5	20%	10%
8	5	5	5	5	Stayed the same	Stayed the same
9	3	3	5	5	40%	40%
10	4	4.5	5	5	20%	10%
11	5	5	5	5	Stayed the same	Stayed the same
12	5	5	3.5	4.5	−30%	−10%
13	4.5	4.5	5	5	10%	10%
14	4	3	4.5	5	10%	40%

The wider impact of forest school

Since beginning the forest school experience, staff have noticed changes in the children's behaviours. Here are examples:

- Children appeared calmer and had fewer outbursts in the forest environment
- Children, who were anxious or lacked concentration in class, seemed calmer and more focused
- A child with medical needs seemed more confident, with notably improved gross motor skills
- Children had increased vocabulary and clearer speech
- Children had a keenness to immerse in the outdoors, even for children who would initially not sit down or touch anything dirty (even though suitable clothing was provided)

Through forest school, children became more resilient; for example, accidental knocks from other children did not cause a problem (as they would in class), and if they tripped or fell, the children tended to join back in without any distress. Other positive aspects were new friendships that emerged, teamwork and the development of gross motor skills as they became apt at walking on uneven ground, climbing trees and using a rope swing. For the children at The Link School, the introduction of forest schooling has re-engaged children back into learning as they experienced a love for the environment. So if you do go down to the woods today, you might not believe your eyes.

Chapter summary

- The role of staff in forest school is to facilitate rather than lead learning
- Connecting with nature and being in the forest environment lead to self-regulation that can transfers positively to the classroom
- Forest school experiences build confidence, self-esteem and resilience, as well as enhance children's academic abilities

- Through forest school, children develop relationships and value the views and opinions of their peers
- Forest school can bring holistic benefits to children's learning and development; and how they interact with other children and the environment around them

 Further reading

Breslin, T. (2021) *Lessons from Lockdown. Lessons from Lockdown. The educational legacy of COVID-19*. London: Routledge.

Cree, J. and Robb, M. (2021) *The essential guide to forest school and nature pedagogy*. London: Routledge.

James, M. (2018) *Forest school and autism: A practical guide*. London: Jessica Kingsley Publishers.

Knight, S. (2016) *Forest school in practice: For all ages*. London: SAGE Publications, Ltd.

Walmsley, N. and Westall, D. (2018) *Forest school adventure. Outdoor skills and play for children*. London: Guild of Master Craftsman Publications.

Worroll, J. and Houghton, P. (2020) *Forest school: Activity cards*. London: Watkins Publishing.

Worroll, J. and Houghton, P. (2021) *Forest school wild play: Outdoor fun with earth, air, fire and water*. London: Watkins Publishing.

References

Cree, J. and Robb, M. (2021) *The essential guide to forest school and nature pedagogy*. New York: Routledge.

Harris, F. (2017) 'The nature of learning at forest school: Practitioners' perspectives', *Education*, 3–13, 45(2), pp. 272–291.

Kellert, S.R. (2005) 'Nature and childhood development', in *Building for life: Designing and understanding the human-nature connection*, edited by S.R. Kellert, 63–89. Washington, DC: Island Press.

Knight, S. (2016) *Forest school in practice, for all ages.* London: SAGE Publications, Ltd.

8 | Engaging and re-engaging children through a managed move or following a school exclusion

Sarah Martin-Denham, Denise Taylor and Donna Walker

This chapter aims to support education providers in re-engaging and integrating CYP following a fixed-period or permanent school exclusion, or a managed-moves process. The case studies in this chapter are based on interviews with caregivers and conversations with CYP as part of a University of Sunderland research commissioned by Together for Children on school exclusions. Denise and Donna, the headteachers of the two provisions involved in the study, provide insight into the approaches they adopted to build relationships and form connections with the CYP and their caregivers to support their participation, learning and achievement.

What is school exclusion?

There are two types of legal school exclusion, introduced through the Education Act 1986, c. 61 – permanent (expelled) and fixed period (suspended), where the child is temporarily removed from the school (DfE, 2021a). Permanent exclusions should only occur in the following circumstances:

*   In response to a serious breach or persistent breaches of the school's behaviour policy

DOI: 10.4324/9781003261506-9

- Where allowing the pupil to remain in school would seriously harm the education or welfare of the pupil or others in the school

(DfE, 2017, p. 10)

The prevalence of school exclusions in England

Permanent school exclusions have been rising since 2012–2013, following a downward trend (DfE, 2018). The 2017/18 data shows that the number of exclusions was higher than in recent years due to increases in NE England (DfE, 2019). Similarly, the 2019/20 data indicate that NE England is the only region with a permanent exclusion rate of 0.1 or higher. The area also has the highest suspension rate, and its secondary school suspension rate (12.95) is considerably higher than the national average (7.43) (DfE, 2021b). Martin-Denham, Donaghue and Benstead (2017) reported that the prevalence of both fixed-period and permanent exclusions in one local area in Sunderland were particularly evident in school years 5, 6, 9 and 10 in the lead up to national assessments. Their findings support national concerns regarding national assessments and the impact of retaining low-attaining children due to published league tables (Gazeley, 2010; House of Commons Education Committee, 2018). In 2018–2019 and 2019–2020, DfE (2020, 2021b) published data noting that pupils with SEND accounted for almost half of all permanent and fixed-period exclusions.

Managed moves

A pupil at any type of school can transfer to another school as part of a 'managed move' where this occurs with the consent of the parties involved, including the parents and the admission authority of the school. However, the threat of exclusion must never be used to influence parents to remove their child from the school.

(DfE, 2017, p. 10)

Research evidence suggests that managed moves are the primary approach to control behaviour as an alternative to permanent school exclusion (Gazeley et al., 2015; Mills and Thomson, 2018; Craggs and Kelly, 2018; Martin-Denham, 2020a). However, despite the DfE (2017) rhetoric that

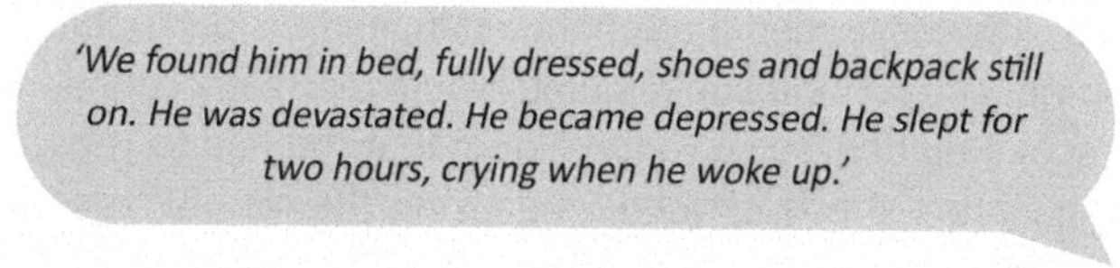

'We found him in bed, fully dressed, shoes and backpack still on. He was devastated. He became depressed. He slept for two hours, crying when he woke up.'

Figure 8.1 Caregiver's reflection on Max's third failed managed move (Martin-Denham, 2020b, p. 64)

parents should not be threatened with exclusion if they don't agree to a managed move, the Children's Commissioner Office (2019) and Hutchinson and Crenna-Jennings (2019) reported contradictory evidence.

The need for recording the success or failure of managed moves is highlighted by Martin- Denham and Donaghue (2020a). Their freedom of information request, responded to by 133 out of 149 local authorities, found that only 53% held data on managed moves, meaning we do not know the extent of the use of managed moves or their success.

> The number attempted by individual children, how many succeed, how many fail, the length of time they sustained the placement and a narrative account of why they failed. This evidence will support a need for a thorough review of the managed move process.
>
> (Martin-Denham and Donaghue, 2020a, p. 7)

Research by Martin-Denham (2020a, 2020b) illustrates the detrimental impact of failed managed moves on children's mental health. Figure 8.1 shares a quote from the caregiver of Max, who had three failed managed moves.

Case study 1: Max

Max (Figure 8.1) was born prematurely, pre-24 weeks gestation. The consultants were unsure whether he would survive. His caregivers were told he might have brain damage, have physical disabilities and be non-verbal. In his early years, Max had multiple surgeries and was described by his caregivers as a loving and caring child. Despite early concerns, he excelled academically during his primary school education, though his teachers reported his behaviour was challenging at times. From the start of secondary school, his mother described a dramatic change in his personality when he was not coping with school. She recalled being frequently called into school about his escalating behaviour to the extent that she had to resign from her job. The behaviours she described as causing the school to summon her were minor misdemeanours, such as low-level disruption in class. Max was not on the SEN register despite his difficulties in school. His mother suggested that the lack of SEN support from his mainstream schools led him to become cannabis dependent. As his cannabis use increased, she requested referrals to CAMHS, CYPS and Early Help but felt no one took responsibility.

> The family was broken. We were broken. Our family has been broken. We are putting it back together a little bit, but it's been horrendous, absolutely horrendous. We were always such a happy family, tried our best, hard workers, grafters. We wanted for nothing, kind and generous to less fortunate people. An ordinary family. Things just got worse and worse, to the point I couldn't believe it.
>
> (Martin-Denham, 2020b, p. 58)

How the AP supported Max

Following admission to AP, several strategies were tried to support Max with his aggressive behaviours. Initially, he would try and abscond when he was upset and angry, and claimed no one understood him. He would often sit in the corridor alone. Relationships are a vital part of the school's ethos, and the corridor was Max's chosen place to begin to form them.

Max started to open up about his worries. Through this, he came to understand why he got angry and accepted that he had a cannabis problem. As the relationship with his key worker developed, he eventually engaged with the Youth, Drug and Alcohol Project (YDAP). At Max's request, the appointments with YDAP were attended with his key worker. The more he was able to trust, the more he accepted the available help. For the first time in a month, his cannabis use began to decrease.

Over time, Max began to flourish; his school attendance increased, and his dysregulated behaviours decreased. As he settled into the routine of school, thoughts turned to his post-16 provision. For the first time in a long time, home and school were synchronised, and the cycle of negative behaviours and blame was broken. Max continued to engage with learning and gained GCSE grades in seven subjects. Through the power of connection, unity and relationships, meaningful changes were made and sustained.

Importance of relationships and creating a sense of belonging

Creating a sense of belonging with children and families is fundamental to wellbeing, healthy development and the successful inclusion of children into education (Maslow, 1943, 1954; Martin-Denham, 2020b). Baumeister and Leary (1995, p. 497) defined a *sense of belonging* as 'a need to form and maintain strong, stable interpersonal relationships', concluding that 'belongingness is a need rather than a want'. This is not a new notion; Bowlby (1969) emphasised how responsive relationships between children and adults allow the creation of positive relationships in later life. Bowlby's work on attachment theory has been developed, highlighting that it is not solely the principal caregiver that children form attachments with; children form multiple attachments as they grow and develop.

Case study 2: Lucy

Lucy took part in the school exclusions research (Martin-Denham, 2020a, 2020b, 2020c). She had attended AP for two years following fixed-period school exclusions from two mainstream secondary schools. She reflected that her difficulties at school were due to uniform breaches and persistent bullying from older children, coupled with mental health needs arising from traumatic episodes in her childhood. Lucy would often be sent to isolation or detention for non-compliance with her uniform and wearing make-up. She described feeling safe in isolation (a small boothed room) and learnt that if she misbehaved, she would get sent out of class to the place of security.

> I used to purposefully get myself put into what was their isolation, to avoid everyone. They used to wait outside of classrooms for me. I used to beg my teachers to let me leave early. They are terrible for bullying.
>
> (Martin-Denham, 2020c, p. 56)

Being isolated affected Lucy's mental health: 'I used to pull my hair out, scratch my face. I couldn't cope with it at all. The teachers used to sit there and watch me cry' (Martin-Denham, 2020c, p. 54).

Lucy reflected on how AP changed her perception of schools, as they listened to her and responded with empathy to her specific needs. Their focus on being part of the 'school family' gave her a sense of belonging and improved her wellbeing and ability to learn.

How the AP school supported Lucy

To support Lucy, the staff team began by getting to know her lived experiences. On arrival, the school quickly formed a strong, trusting relationship with Lucy's mother and stepfather through conversations. Her mother had a history of life-limiting illnesses since Lucy's premature birth, which had resulted in Lucy's father becoming estranged from the family early in Lucy's life. During Lucy's childhood, she was exposed to a wide range of traumatic ACEs, including physical assaults from peers. Lucy was fortunate that there was a very supportive family environment at home, and the strategies developed during the time she was a student at the school were formed in partnership between home and school. This constant communication and joint approach to support was key in guiding Lucy and supporting her SEMH needs.

Lucy was drawn to abusive, controlling relationships where she felt she could make a difference and save the other person from their issues. At the time of joining the school, Lucy was in a relationship with known patterns of domestic abuse. When this relationship ended, Lucy began a relationship with an older male (a victim of sexual assault) where she would physically assault him. Over time, Lucy was able to articulate how her experience of these relationships affected her ability to form and maintain female friendship groups, as she had an inappropriate perception of what a healthy relationship should be. Stress and anxiety led to self-harm, suicide ideation, erratic mental health and anger, increasing to a point where she would verbalise an irrational desire to kill someone.

One-to-one counselling was put in place from the first week, giving Lucy a named point of contact with whom she felt safe and comfortable to talk to. Several external agencies were instrumental in offering wraparound care, so Lucy was effectively supported inside and outside school. Early Help, CYPS, Family Therapy and Bright Futures all contributed to the network of agencies that had Lucy and the family's best interests at heart.

A considerable number of resources were devoted to ensuring Lucy had space and time to talk in school. Protected time for staff to listen to Lucy was essential in providing the right level of support. Art proved a hugely positive focus and an outlet for Lucy, who is very creative (Figure 8.2). The art room and a sketchbook provided a calming space for Lucy to de-stress, think and create some amazing pieces, often responding to mental health concerns or relaying positive messages to others.

Lucy became a respected and valued member of the school community, from the point of view of both staff and students, and she regularly advised and contributed on behalf of the other students about whole-school policies and strategies. She was highly articulate and mature beyond her years, and it was fantastic to watch her confidence and independence grow as time progressed. Lucy successfully moved into an apprenticeship post-16 and made us extremely proud.

The importance of relationships and a sense of belonging

There is broad recognition and acceptance of the Neurosequential Model of Therapeutics, which highlights that relationships are the fundamental basis for any successful therapeutic intervention and for resilience building to manage self-control, behaviour and learning (Hambrick et al., 2018). Holmes (2001), Cairns (2002) and Gerhardt (2004) agree that to thrive, children need interpersonal support through significant others who are reliable, stable, attentive, friendly and empathetic. Shonkoff (2017) advocated children need responsive relationships to build healthy brain architecture and a well-regulated response system (something that Perry (2016) recognised). The DfE (2016, p. 8) acknowledges a sense of belonging as a protective factor in building resilience, stating, 'schools should be a safe and affirming place for children, where they can develop a sense of belonging and feel able to trust and talk openly with adults about their problems'.

Figure 8.2 A piece of Lucy's artwork

Extensive studies have shown that a positive sense of belonging has associations with good mental health and positivity about the future (Van Ryzin, Gravely and Roseth, 2009; Kidger et al., 2012; Marraccini and Brier, 2017; Martin-Denham, 2020b), resulting in a positive and influential effect on children's emotional, motivational and academic functioning (Craggs and Kelly, 2018).

The potential risks of engagement with statutory education

This section outlines the potential risks to the child, family or school following a fixed-period or permanent school exclusion (Table 8.1). It is likely that children will already have had extensive periods of absence during

Table 8.1 Child, family and school barriers to successful re-integration to school

Theme	Barrier to re-integration
Child-specific risks	
Cannot attend school	The child may be 'unable to go' to school due to their SEMH needs.
Disrupted sleep patterns	The child may have had unusual sleep patterns due to being away from the school routine. Reasons for this include not feeling safe in school or having age-stage development for adolescents.
Mental health difficulties returning or being compounded	Long periods of absence from school may compound attachment difficulties at home and school. These could arise due to pressure to catch up on lost learning, or previous or recent traumatic experiences. However, it must be recognised that being in school is a significant negative factor on the SEMH of some children. These CYP actively seek to be excluded to remove themselves from school.
Responding to the level of support needed	Children who have been excluded from school have a loss of routine, structure, friendship, opportunity and freedom.
Increased risk of low self-esteem/ self-confidence	There is a risk the child will have difficulty with the level/volume of school work due to missed schooling.

(Continued)

Table 8.1 (Continued) Child, family and school barriers to successful re-integration to school

Theme	Barrier to re-integration
Family-specific risks	
Impact of the child not being able to attend school	The effects on the family of a child unable to return to school can include loss of employment, fines, court or increased stress within the household. There may be changes to family circumstances where they may now be entitled to financial support but have not applied.
Impact on other children within the household	The impact of a child anxious about returning to school could be observed by other children in the household, increasing their anxieties about schooling and replicating behaviours or withdrawing. If a child at home displays childhood challenging, violent or aggressive behaviour (CCVAB), the sibling may have been exposed to higher levels of household domestic violence.
Impact on caregiver's mental health	The impact on the mental health of family members as they establish boundaries and support the transition to school, particularly where there are incidents of CCVAB. If the child feels unable to attend, this may impact all relationships within the family unit.
Dealing with expectations and involvement of professionals	The impact on mental health and ability to maintain employment due to the number of contacts and requests for attending appointments in schools and with other multi-agency professionals.
The risks for schools	
Accommodating the range of transition needs	Many children will need to return on flexible timetables, with risk assessments for health and safety. Some children will need access to safe spaces, where they can go should they feel overwhelmed.
Increased need for training	Staff training may be needed to understand and respond appropriately to new or re-emerging behaviours following a school exclusion. A range of interventions may need to be considered rather than relying on a limited number of approaches.
League tables	Impact on the attainment of missed schooling and, therefore, league tables.

COVID-19, compounding their barriers to engaging or re-engaging with schooling. The term 'unable to go to school' is used instead of the frequently used term 'school refusal' (Square Peg, 2021). For many children, it is not that they refuse to go to school, but rather, they are unable to, due to SEMH needs – some of which were brought about due to traumatic experiences in education.

The re-integration model

The integration model is an adaptation of the Martin-Denham (2020a) managed-move model, based on her research on school exclusion. The model (Figure 8.3) shares an approach to support the transition and integration of children following a permanent exclusion and move to a new school or as part of the managed-move process. The model has six distinct and essential steps:

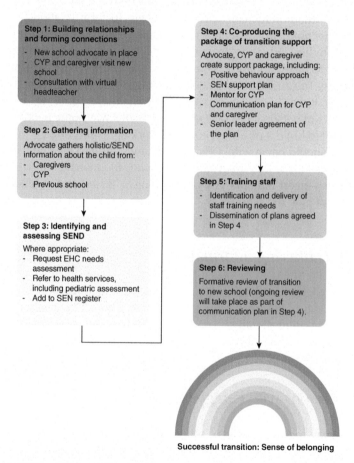

Figure 8.3 The re-integration model
Adapted from Martin-Denham (2020a)

Step 1: Building relationships and forming connections

The SENCO or pastoral lead (herein referred to as 'advocate') may be best placed to lead step 1. It begins when the receiving school is approached for the new placement and the current school, caregiver and child agree. For cared for children, the designated teacher and virtual headteacher also need to be consulted on the planned transition to a new school. The role of the advocate is to build positive relationships between the child, caregiver and school (Martin-Denham, 2020a) to begin to form relationships and make connections. It is essential to recognise that relationships are such between families and school team members that negative relationships can be formed. As professionals, it is crucial to recognise when relationships are not working. The advocate may need to change to prevent any detriment to either party. It should not be seen as a personal failure – at times, there can be a conflict of personalities or a range of reasons why some people find it challenging to build a positive, proactive working relationship.

Step 1 should begin with a visit to the new school so the child and caregiver can decide if they wish to proceed with the managed move. Some children may need multiple visits, beginning with seeing the school and meeting staff after the school day.

Step 2: Gathering information

The purpose is to provide schools with crucial information to effectively plan for and meet the needs of children entering their school. Caregivers, CYP and the previous school should be approached to share information to ensure a holistic picture of the child's views, wishes, feelings and learning barriers.

Conversations with caregiver(s)

Families may feel very wary of school staff due to their previous experiences of meetings or working with schools. The advocate should ask the caregiver(s) where they would feel most comfortable meeting and be considerate of their work/care commitments. Some caregivers will answer all

12–18 questions in Table 8.2 in one discussion; others may need the conversations over time.

Table 8.2 Indicative questions to ask caregiver(s)

Question number	Question
1	How are you today?
2	How would you describe (child's name)?
3	Is there anything you feel we should know at home that could help us support (child's name)?
4	Apart from someone like the health visitor who visits all new mums and babies, has (child's name) been part of any other support services? If yes: Can you give me an idea of when this was (from-to)? Are they still working with you now? (Early Help / Children's Social Care / Police)
5	What do you feel were the problems (child's name) was having at school?
6	Does your child have any diagnosed SEND?
7	Do you think your child has any undiagnosed SEND?
8	What do you feel we could do to help (child's name) settle into school?
9	Are you concerned about the behaviour change you have seen?
10	Do you feel there might be any changes in (child's name) when they start school again?
11	Is there anything you feel might help you support them with the changes you have seen in their behaviour?
12	Is there anything else you would like to tell me? Do you have any questions you would like to ask?
Additional questions	
13	Can you tell me who their social worker is?
14	Do you know if they have any siblings they are not currently living with?
15	Do you know how many moves they have had since coming into the care system?
16	Do you know what support the Virtual School Team has provided since they came into the care system?
17	Can you tell me what post-adoption support you have had, if any, for yourself, your family and (child's name)?
18	Do you know if they have been assessed or seen by anyone to find out what support might be helpful for them?

Conversations with CYP

As with caregivers, CYP may also be wary of school staff due to their prior experiences in school. The child should be consulted on how the introductions to the advocate occur (Table 8.3), and their caregiver should accompany the child. They may wish for a significant adult from the previous/current school to attend, where sought; this should be arranged.

Gathering information from the previous or current school

The information the advocate receives from schools will vary, depending on the effectiveness of their systems and processes. Table 8.4 provides critical questions to ask the SENCO or pastoral staff at the CYP's current or previous school.

The second part is general questions relating to the child's experiences during their previous school placements. These questions should be asked with a trusted adult in a setting suited to the caregiver(s). Careful consideration needs to be given to how these questions are asked, as some will have experienced traumatic events. The questions are not an exhaustive list but a guide.

Table 8.3 Indicative questions to ask CYP

Question number	Question
1	What kinds of things did you like to do at school?
2	Can you tell me how you feel about going back to school?
3	Was there anything that worried you when you were at your school?
4	What was the work like at school? Was there anything you felt was quite tricky or hard to do?
5	Was there anything you felt was easy to do?
6	What do you think might help you when you come to this school?

Table 8.4 Indicative questions to ask the previous or current school

Question number	Question
About the child	
1	What are the child's strengths?
2	What are the child's interests?
3	What are the child's aspirations?
4	What are the child's barriers to participation and learning?
5	What would support their transition to a new school?
6	Is there an adult in the school they have a good relationship with?
7	Does the child have a history of struggling to come to school?
8	Are they eligible for FSMs and does the child use them?
9	Has their FSM status changed during their time in your school?
10	Is the child entitled to previously LAC, pupil premium or Armed Services PP?
Relationships with the caregiver(s)	
11	How would you describe your relationship with the child and caregivers?
12	Have they been subject to any formal attendance procedures?
SEND history	
13	Can you tell me their SEND history?
14	What is the child's primary, secondary and other additional needs?
15	Did the child's SEND status change during school?
Identification and assessment	
16	What internal and external assessments were carried out and by whom? What was the outcome?
External agency involvement	
17	Is there currently any agency involvement?
18	What internal and external support did the child and caregivers receive?
19	What follow-up work needs to occur through Early Help, CiN or CPPs? Who is involved and who needs to be contacted?
Special educational provision (SEP)	
20	What specific interventions were in place in school?
21	Can you share the previous two years of SEN support plans and reviews?
22	Was an EHCP being considered/applied for?
23	What reasonable adjustments were in place?
24	What exam access arrangements were in place?
Medical needs	
25	Is there an individual health care plan in place? When was it last updated?
26	Does the child have any chronic medical conditions that impact how often they attend school?
Looking ahead	
27	What do you feel are the support needs for the child and family moving forward?

Step 3: Identifying and assessing SEND

Using the information gathered in step 2, the advocate may need to lead on the identification and assessment of SEND. An application for an EHC needs assessment may be required if the child meets the legal test (see Chapter 1). Referrals may be required for the CYP for a sight/hearing test, a paediatric assessment or support/assessment from broader health services.

Step 4: Co-producing the package of transition support

The purpose of step 2 is to provide the new school with crucial information to effectively pre-plan for the CYP's transition to their new setting. Once the information is gathered, the advocate creates a support package in collaboration with the caregivers and CYP. This will detail the following:

- Pastoral supports the CYP will receive
- Positive behaviour that will be promoted and celebrated, and how/when any sanctions will be imposed
- Suggested SEN support plan, outlining SEP with SMART targets
- Mentor for the CYP to be their point of contact for any issues arising in the school day
- Support, where appropriate, for the application for an EHC needs assessment
- Communication plan (how and when the caregiver and child will receive updates (daily/weekly) on how the transition is progressing and how concerns will be addressed)

Before signing off, the Senior Leadership Team should meet with the advocate, caregiver and child (where appropriate) to agree on the proposed support package.

Step 5: Training staff

This step utilises the information gathered in the previous steps to identify any training needs in the staff team in preparation for the transition of the

CYP to the school. Training will be needed when the CYP has SEND that the school may be unfamiliar with, and the support package agreed in step 2 needs to be disseminated. All staff need to be made aware of the support in place to apply the co-produced reasonable adjustments in accordance with the Equality Act 2010. Staff training may also be needed to address the stigma of children excluded from school and to share the communication plan.

Step 6: Reviewing

Once the CYP is in the new school, a review will be needed periodically. These should be set out and shared with caregivers and the CYP

Chapter summary

A successful transition between schools relies on securing positive relationships and a sense of belonging in the new school. When a child has been excluded from school, relationships are often irretrievably broken. It will take time for both children and caregivers to heal and for trust to embed. If a school can know and understand the CYP's holistic needs, this information can be used to plan for their transition. The authors believe that there is a greater chance of a successful outcome through co-producing the transition plan with the schools, caregivers and CYP.

 Further reading

Martin-Denham, S. (2020a) *The enablers and barriers to mainstream schooling: The voices of children excluded from school, their caregivers, and professionals.* Sunderland: University of Sunderland.

Martin-Denham, S. (2020b) *The enablers and barriers to successful managed moves: The voice of children, caregivers, and professionals.* Sunderland: University of Sunderland.

Martin-Denham, S. (2020c) *A review of school exclusion on the mental health, well-being of children and young people in the City of Sunderland*. Sunderland: University of Sunderland.

Martin-Denham, S. (2020d) 'Riding the rollercoaster of school exclusion coupled with drug misuse: The lived experience of caregivers', *Emotional and Behavioural Difficulties*, 25(3–4), pp. 244–263. doi:1 0.1080/13632752.2020.1848985.

Martin-Denham, S. (2021a) *Alternative approaches to school exclusion: Perspectives of headteachers in England*. Sunderland: University of Sunderland.

Martin-Denham, S. (2021b) *The benefits of school exclusion: Research with headteachers in England*. Sunderland: University of Sunderland.

Martin-Denham, S. (2021c) 'Defining, identifying, and recognising underlying causes of social, emotional, and mental health difficulties: Thematic analysis of interviews with headteachers in England', *Emotional and Behavioural Difficulties*, pp. 1–19. doi:10.1080/13632752. 2021.1930909.

Martin-Denham, S. (2021d) 'School exclusion, substance misuse and use of weapons: An interpretative phenomenological analysis of interviews with children', *Support for Learning*, 36(4), pp. 532–554. doi:10.1111/1467-9604.12379.

Martin-Denham, S. (2021e) 'The varying alternatives to school exclusion: Interviews with headteachers in England', *Emotional and Behavioural Difficulties*' [In production]. doi:10.1080/13632752.20 21.1983326.

Martin-Denham, S. and Donaghue, J. (2020a) *Excluded for no real reason: What is the extent of the use of the category 'other' in school census returns in England? A policy brief*. Sunderland: University of Sunderland.

Martin-Denham, S. and Donaghue, J. (2020b) *Out of sight, out of mind? Managed moves in England*. Sunderland: University of Sunderland.

Martin-Denham, S. and Watts, S. (2019) *SENCO handbook: Leading provision and practice*. London: SAGE Publications, Ltd.

References

Baumeister, R. and Leary, M. (1995) 'The need to belong: Desire for interpersonal attachments as a fundamental human motivation', *Psychological Bulletin*, 117, pp. 497–529.

Bowlby, J. (1969) *Attachment and loss: Volume 1. Attachment.* New York: Basic Books.

Cairns, K. (2002) *Attachment, trauma and resilience.* London: British Association for Adoption and Fostering.

Children's Commissioner Office (2019) *Exclusions from mainstream schools.* Available at: https://www. childrenscommissioner.gov.uk/publication/exclusions-from-mainstream-schools/ (Accessed: 4 November 2021).

Craggs, H. And Kelly, C. (2018) 'School belonging: Listening to the voice of secondary school students who have undergone managed moves', *School Psychology International'*, 39(1), pp. 56–73.

Department of Education (DfE) (2016) *Behaviour and discipline in schools: Advice for headteachers and school staff.* London: DfE.

DfE (2017) *Exclusion from maintained schools, academies and pupil referral units in England Statutory guidance for those with legal responsibilities in relation to exclusion.* London: DfE.

DfE (2018) *Permanent and fixed-period exclusions in England: 2016–2017.* London: DfE.

DfE (2019) *Permanent and fixed-period exclusions in England: 2017 to 2018.* London: DfE.

DfE (2020) *Permanent and fixed-period exclusions in England: 2018 to 2019.* London: DfE.

DfE (2021a) *School discipline and exclusions.* Available at: https://www.gov.uk/school-discipline-exclusions/exclusions (Accessed: 6 November 2021).

DfE (2021b) *Permanent and fixed-period exclusions in England: 2019 to 2020.* London: DfE.

Education Act 1986, c. 61. Available at: https://www.legislation.gov.uk/ukpga/1986/61/pdfs/ukpga_19860061_en.pdf (Accessed: 6 November 2021).

Gazeley, L. (2010) 'The role of school exclusion processes in the reproduction of social and educational disadvantage', *British Journal of Educational Studies*, 58(3), pp. 293–309.

Gazeley, L. et al. (2015) 'Contextualising inequalities in rates of school exclusion in English Schools: Beneath the "Tip of the Ice-Berg"', *British Journal of Educational Studies*, 63(4), pp. 487–504. doi:10.10 80/00071005.2015.1070790.

Gerhardt, S. (2004) *Why love matters*. London: Brunner Routledge.

Hambrick, E.P. et al. (2018) 'Restraint and critical incident reduction following introduction of the neurosequential model of therapeutics', *Residential Treatment for Children and Youth*, 35(1), pp. 2–23.

Holmes, J. (2001) *The search for a secure base*. Hove: Brunner-Routledge.

House of Commons Education Committee (2018) *Forgotten children: Alternative provision and the scandal of ever-increasing exclusions: Fifth report of session 2017–19*. London: House of Commons.

Hutchinson, J. and Crenna-Jennings, W. (2019) *Unexplained pupil exits from schools*. London: Education Policy Institute.

Kidger, J., Araya, R., Donovan, J. and Gunnell, D. (2012) 'The Effect of the School Environment on the Emotional Health of Adolescents: A Systematic Review', *Pediatrics*, 129(5), pp. 925–949. doi:10.1542/peds.2011-2248.

Marraccini, M.E. and Brier, Z.M.F. (2017) 'School connectedness and suicidal thoughts and behaviors: A systematic meta-analysis.', *School Psychology Quarterly*, 32(1), pp. 5–21. doi:10.1037/spq0000192.

Martin-Denham, S. (2020a) *The enablers and barriers to successful managed moves: The voice of children, caregivers and professionals*. Sunderland: University of Sunderland.

Martin-Denham, S. (2020b) *A review of school exclusion on the mental health, wellbeing of children and young people in the City of Sunderland*. Sunderland: University of Sunderland.

Martin-Denham, S. (2020c) *The enablers and barriers to mainstream schooling: The voices of children excluded from school, their caregivers, and professionals*. Sunderland: University of Sunderland.

Martin-Denham, S., Donaghue, J. and Benstead, H. (2017) *The prevalence of special educational needs and disabilities (SEND) identified in young people, aged 3–16, across the City of Sunderland.* Sunderland: University of Sunderland.

Maslow, A. (1943) 'A theory of human motivation', *Psychological Review*, 50(4), pp. 370–396.

Maslow, A. (1954) *Motivation and personality.* New York: Harper and Row.

Mills, M. and Thomson, P. (2018) *Investigative research into alternative provision.* London: DfE.

Perry, B. (2016) *The brain science behind student trauma.* Available at: https://www.edweek.org/ew/articles/2016/12/14/the-brain-science-behind-student-trauma.html (Accessed: 11 May 2020).

Shonkoff, J.P. (2017) 'Breakthrough impacts', *Young Children*, 72(2), pp. 8–16.

Square Peg (2021) *'Please can we banish the term 'school refusal'.* Available at: https://www.sendgateway.org.uk/blog/square-peg-please-can-we-banish-term-school-refusal (Accessed: 3 December 2021).

Van Ryzin, M.J., Gravely, A.A. and Roseth, C.J. (2009) 'Autonomy, Belongingness, and Engagement in School as Contributors to Adolescent Psychological Well-Being', *Journal of Youth and Adolescence*, 38(1), pp. 1–12. doi:10.1007/s10964-007-9257-4.

9 | Co-production with children and young people and their caregivers in alternative provision

Kerrie Whelan and Dominick Gray

This chapter shares a hypothetical case study of Ned. It combines the views of two headteachers from NE England and shares what would be their approach to re-integrating Ned into education. Their schools are Endeavour Academy and The Beacon Centre, which are APs that educate and care for CYP who are unable to manage in a mainstream setting for reasons, such as being unable to go to school, having challenging behaviour or being at risk of or being excluded.

Endeavour academy

The school provides for KS4 CYP experiencing SEMH difficulties. Endeavour Academy commissions places for CYP who have missed large amounts of schooling due to illness, for CYP where the school has exhausted all strategies to re-engage, or for those at risk of disengagement or exclusion after demonstrating behaviour linked with anxiety. Pupil premium was significantly above average for 2018/19 (83%), although this fluctuates as admissions occur throughout the academic year. The CYP are predominantly white British, with English as their first language.

 DOI: 10.4324/9781003261506-10

The Beacon Centre

The Beacon Centre in South Tyneside offers places for CYP between 4 and 16 years of age who have been permanently excluded from school. In 2020/21, the most common reasons for school suspensions were drug- and alcohol-related (26%), or physical assault against a CYP or adult (17%). Almost 20% of pupils have an EHCP with SEMH as the primary need. A further 10% of the CYP are awaiting a final decision on whether they will be granted an EHCP. In the primary provision, the vast majority of CYP are boys, compared to just over half in the secondary school site. The proportion of disadvantaged CYP is considerably higher than the national average, with 69% eligible for FSMs, compared to 20.8% nationally (DfE, 2021). Most CYP at the school are white British, and 7% are cared for children.

Why children get referred to AP

Most students who are referred to AP have experienced a previous managed move (see Chapter 8) or school exclusion. In a report by The Education Policy Institute, Hutchinson and Crenna-Jennings (2019) estimated that, in 2017, roughly one in eight (12.8%) of all unexplained exits from school were accounted for by managed moves (p. 19). In total, 14.7 pupils per 1,000 in the 2017 cohort experienced a managed move at some point in their secondary school career (IntegratED, 2020). Hutchinson and Crenna-Jennings noted that these figures are 'not perfect' (p. 19), and Martin-Denham and Donaghue (2020) found that schools are not required to record managed moves nor do they on a consistent basis.

During the COVID-19 pandemic, a survey of 5,000 caregivers of children with SEND reported higher levels of stress due to their child's behaviour (Waite et al., 2020). Parentkind found that 92% of parents had an 'overwhelmingly negative experience' when talking to their child's headteacher about their school exclusion, with only 6% referred for additional help by their child's school (Parentkind, 2018). The Parentkind Report (2018) also reported that just over half of all caregivers who responded to their survey were not aware of their school's exclusions policy prior to their child's exclusion.

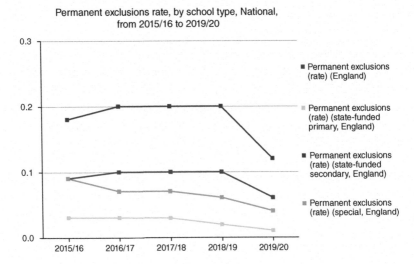

Figure 9.1 Permanent exclusions rates
Source: DfE (2020)

The national picture: permanent school exclusions

In 2019, 7,894 pupils were permanently excluded from school, equating to a permanent exclusion rate of 1.0 per 1,000 pupils (IntegratED Annual Report, 2020). Figure 9.1 illustrates the number of permanent school exclusion rates by type of school from 2015/16 to 2019/20.

Support the needs of CYP with SEND

Staff presence and positioning are imperative to setting the tone for the school day. Meeting CYP on arrival each morning, as they hand in their mobile phones, provides an opportunity to assess the range of emotions they are presenting with. Through being present at the start of the day, interventions can take place promptly before they begin formalised learning. In a small school, the staff can quickly be informed to monitor and check in on CYP's wellbeing throughout the day to make sure their mood is stabilised.

Case study: Ned

This section shares a hypothetical narrative case study of Ned and his pathway to school exclusion, to illustrate common issues and how connections with the CYP and caregiver are or are not established and maintained. While we can question what support could have been offered and at what point, the focus needs to be on how to move forward. The theograph (Figure 9.2 and Table 9.1) illustrates his pathway to school exclusion.

About Ned

Ned was 15 years old and the youngest of four children. His mother was often bedridden with complex health issues, and his father was the main caregiver. Both caregivers were unemployed and struggled financially to meet the family's basic needs.

Nursery

Ned attended morning sessions at nursery. The staff shared with his father that he had difficulty sharing toys and would distance himself from other children. Also, during story time, Ned was observed to be unsettled and fidgety, requiring them to often remind him to settle and sit still.

Infant and junior school

During his time in the infant school, Ned continued to be alone at playtimes and was reluctant to engage with staff when attempts were made to encourage him to join games. Academically, Ned made good progress, and no concerns were shared with his caregivers.

In junior school, issues began to occur immediately. The behaviours Ned displayed included pushing tables and lashing out at other children. The school SENCO referred for an educational psychologist assessment. Following their recommendations, Ned was placed in a nurture group provision, where he remained for the duration of junior school. In the nurture provision,

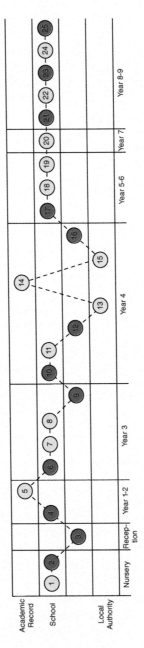

Figure 9.2 Theograph of Ned's journey

Table 9.1 Commentary of Ned's journey

#	Event	#	Event
1	Ned began morning sessions at nursery.	9	The school struggles to get the caregivers to come in for meetings. The mother stated it was due to health needs and commitments with the other children.
2	Teacher raised concern to caregiver (not sharing toys or preferring being alone). Statutory assessments identifying strengths and learning needs carried out; feedback given to caregivers but no indication of any support offered.	10	Ned's teachers believe he is beginning to stand out from peers, with staff describing him as being a loner.
3	Teachers report concerns to caregivers – Ned is unsettled and fidgets. Information passed to primary school and was discussed during transition. No referrals.	11	School carries out a home visit to discuss behaviour concerns with caregivers.
4	Ned observed being alone at playtimes. He appears reluctant to engage with staff when attempts are made to encourage him to join games.	12	The home is described as unorganised, untidy and overcrowded. His mother is sleeping downstairs due to ill health. Caregivers suspected of having possible learning needs.
5	Academically, Ned is making progress, and no concerns with learning are documented.	13	A referral is made to social care and health due to concerns relating to parenting and unsuitable home conditions.
6	Ned transitioned from infant to junior school and struggled to settle. Other children comment, saying he is different. Ned isolates himself more from peers.	14	School attendance is described as excellent. Academically, he is average for his age.
7	Teacher provides a buddy to encourage Ned to socialise. Staff make a conscious effort to include Ned in break time games with lunchtime supervisors asked to keep an eye out for Ned.	15	Family support from children's social care provided to caregivers to enable structure at home and to access services to support the mother's health needs.
8	Ned is given the role of working in the school library over break time. Ned is reported to really enjoy this.	16	The family moved out of area.

(Continued)

Table 9.1 (Continued) Commentary of Ned's journey

#	Event	#	Event
17	Ned is admitted to a new primary school where issues immediately begin to occur. Ned is physically aggressive (pushing and lashing out) towards staff and children.	22	Year 8 (spring) – a managed move is initiated, and after a trial period, Ned transfers to the new school permanently.
18	The SENCO refers to educational psychology for assessment. School considers applying for an education health care needs assessment.	23	Year 9 (autumn) – an incident in the schoolyard over lunchtime results in a permanent exclusion.
19	On the educational psychologist's recommendation, Ned is placed in a nurture group or unit provision within the school. A referral was made to occupational therapy. He responds well to nurture provision and continues to make academic progress.	24	Ned is placed in a Pupil Referral Unit.
20	Ned transitions to mainstream secondary school. Following the transition support and work carried out between the primary SENCO and secondary transition lead, Ned is placed in the secondary year 7 nurture group.	25	Ned was permanently excluded from the Pupil Referral Unit.
21	During years 8 and 9, Ned's attendance and behaviour declines. Ned distracts other CYP, requires constant supervision and is sent out of class due to aggressive behaviours. Ned was not making expected progress and struggled to form friendships.		

Ned struggled to settle and isolated himself from other children, who commented that Ned was different. In response, the staff implemented a buddy to encourage Ned to socialise with other children and made a conscious effort to include him in break time games with lunchtime supervisors. Ned was given a role of responsibility, working in the school library during break times.

Despite trying, the school struggled to get caregivers to attend meetings. In year 4, Ned was beginning to stand out from peers, with staff describing him as being a loner. The school carried out a home visit to discuss concerns with caregivers. They described the family home as 'unorganised, untidy and overcrowded', as his mother was sleeping downstairs due to her disabilities.

Based solely on the home visit, the staff thought both Ned's caregivers had learning disabilities. Due to their concerns, the designated safeguarding officer made a referral to children's social care and health services. Throughout his junior schooling, Ned's attendance was described as excellent, and he was academically average for his age. In year 6, the family moved area.

Secondary school

On admission to mainstream secondary school, Ned was placed in the year 7 nurture group. During years 8 and 9, his attendance declined and his behaviour was reported as a concern. Teachers reported Ned was as follows:

- Distracting others
- Requiring constant supervision
- Refusing to complete work
- Being sent out of class and spending most days in the learning support base

Ned was no longer making academic progress and he was struggling to form friendships. His school uniform appeared grubby and worn. In year 8, Ned had a successful managed move to a new school. In year 9, an incident in the schoolyard led to Ned being permanently excluded.

AP

Ned was placed into a Pupil Referral Unit but was permanently excluded shortly after. He re-started his schooling at Endeavour Academy.

Forming a connection and relationship with Ned and his mother

Using the information provided in the case study, the theograph (Figure 9.2) and the table (Table 9.1), consider the following reflective activity.

> ### REFLECTIVE ACTIVITY
>
> - When were Ned's learning needs assessed and identified?
> - Was it a problem that Ned preferred to be alone at playtimes?
> - What assessments (and by whom) could have supported Ned and his family?
> - What interventions could have supported Ned?
> - What support do you think the family needed?
> - What might the family need in the future?

Making Every Contact Count (MECC)

A chance encounter on an NHS training programme led to the most effective teaching programme we have in Endeavour. In 2018, the deputy head-teacher attended the Making Every Contact Count (MECC) training, where the emphasis is to use every interaction as an intervention. For example, should someone attend a maternity appointment and be found to be smoking, then the staff were being trained to signpost to smoking cessation. They considered how this approach could work in a school setting. The Endeavour approach to MECC involves making a difference to someone's day by doing the following:

- Saying 'good morning' as you pass staff and other young people
- Holding a door open
- Letting someone on the bus before you
- Making a cup of tea for a caregiver or a member of staff at the end of the school day

Lessons that teach resilience, MECC and restorative approaches are embedded into the core and hidden curriculum. For many of our young people, the act of apologising can be difficult. By making a member of staff a cup of tea at the end of the school day, you are more likely to begin to repair the relationship than using isolation or detention.

At Endeavour Academy, all staff wear the MECC questions on their lanyards (Figure 9.3). The staff frame their questions as 'why have you done this?' and more 'what is happening to make you feel this way?' and 'what can we do to help?' Consider the benefits of this approach.

Supporting Ned's transition

Before admission to the school and the admission meeting (Table 9.2), it is recommended you follow the Martin-Denham (2020) re-integration model shared in Chapter 8. Before formally beginning the transition process, Ned and his father were invited for a tour of the school to alleviate any feelings or anxieties. Following the tour, they were signposted to the school website and Facebook page. The purpose of signposting was to share a typical day at the school and to support them to feel a sense of belonging. When meeting with CYP and caregivers, it is important to consider where you have the first conversation (home, school or a relaxed or formal space).

The following section shares how Ned was integrated into AP.

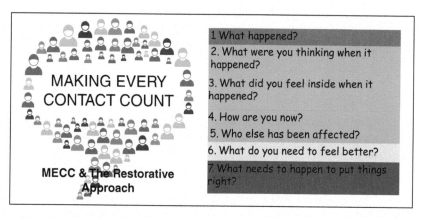

Figure 9.3 The Endeavour Academy lanyard

Step 1. The admission meeting

The purpose of the admission meeting was to have an informal conversation with Ned and his mother to put them at ease and understand their views, wishes and feelings.

Often, caregivers (and CYP) arrive at the admission meeting with preconceived opinions of APs – but once these are discussed and a tour of the school is complete, they leave the initial meeting feeling more positive about their child's path through education, due to the ability of APs to offer increased individual and bespoke approaches to develop the emotional resilience of the CYP.

Table 9.2 The process of leading an admission meeting

Step	The process
1	Invite Ned and his father to share 'what happened in the last school and why?' Sensitively explore the reasons for the school exclusion. The CYP may solely focus on the last negative incident that happened before the exclusion. Caregivers may feel the reason was due to staff or several members that 'had it in for them'.
2	Discuss their right to appeal the permanent school exclusion. Often caregivers and CYP will not wish to appeal the permanent exclusion due to lack of confidence in the mainstream school and the strong desire for a fresh start.
3	

Figure 9.4 Ned's views and feelings about his previous school

4	Ask Ned and his father to reflect on implications of the exclusion/transition on other family members.
5	In collaboration with Ned and his father, discuss and agree on the timeframes for transition to the new provision.
6	Take a photograph of the CYP so they feel a part of the school community.
7	Explain the SNAP B questionnaire (see later) 'at home'. Emphasise that there is no judgement regarding their parenting and an honest approach will ensure that Ned receives a bespoke emotional wellbeing recovery programme through the creation of a comprehensive profile (Figures 9.5, 9.6 and 9.7 – examples of SNAP B profile).

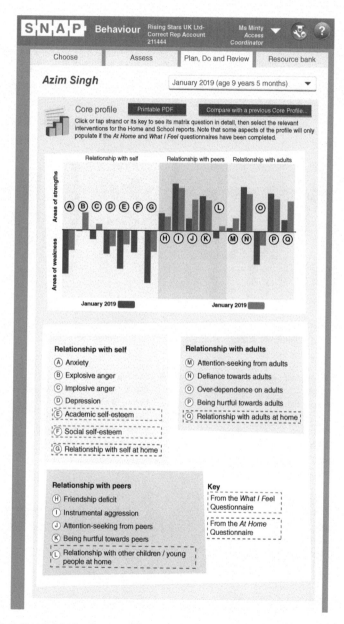

Figure 9.5 SNAP B behaviour profile
(Hodder Education, 2019)

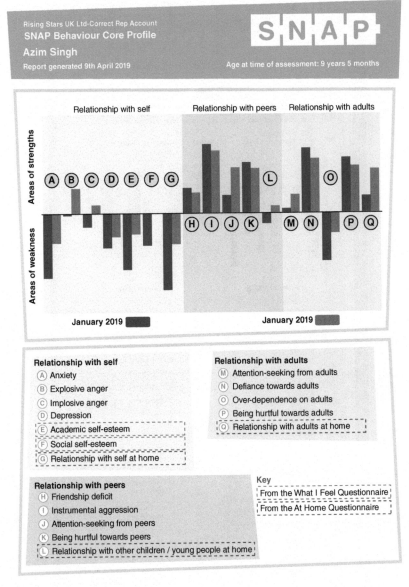

Figure 9.6 SNAP B assessment report
(Hodder Education, 2019)

Azim Singh	SNAP Behaviour Core Profile	S N A P
Report generated 9th April 2019	Age at time of assessment: 9 years 5 months	

Area of strength and weakness

Below are listed Azim's strongest areas, and the 3 areas in which he could most improve.

Principal strengths

SNAP-Behaviour suggest that Azim has strength in:

- **Responding challenge,** which means that he can manage frustrations and use problem-solving skills, instead of aggression, when faced with challenges.
- **Reacting towards adults,** which means that he is cooperative and helpful with adults and accepts directions and reprimands from them calmly.
- **Attitudes towards adults,** which means that he is respectful and can maintain positive relationshps with adults, and can accept being corrected.

Principal weakness

SNAP-Behaviour suggests that Azim's might be affected by:

- **Poor relationship with self at home,** which means that he may suffer with self-doubts about his abilities and does not belive he can improve things through his own efforts.
- **Anxiety,** which means that he will quickly give up or run away from situations with which he cannot cope. He may try to over-control situations in order to avoid anxiety.
- **Low academic self-esteem,** which means that he may have a negative attitude towards his learning and can often be worried about his schoolwork. He may expect to fail when faced with new learning challenges.

Figure 9.7 SNAP B behaviour core profile
(Hodder Education, 2019)

Step 2. Week 1

During the first week of school, Ned completed his version of the SNAP B assessment, 'all about me' (Hodder Education, 2019). The SNAP B profile was shared with Ned and his father, highlighting areas of strength and identified barriers to learning. Using the SNAP B assessment and other school-based information, personalised strategies were discussed with the father to support Ned in the family home. Next, Ned completed a pupil portrait, asking what he felt staff need to know about him (Figure 9.8).

A couple of months into year 10 I was referred to Alternative Provision as I was not attending my old school at all. I missed most of year 9 as I faked being ill every morning so that I didn't have to go.

In my old school I was struggling with communicating with people and my mental health was bad everyday, as I didn't communicate well I was suffering in silence. In lessons the classes were too big and too loud so I couldn't concentrate and didn't get any work done. I am the kind of learner who enjoys working in a classroom with a group of people that isn't too loud and isn't too quiet so that I can just get on with my work. In corridors when switching to a different lesson I really struggled as there was a lot of people in a tight space. The mainstream environment was not for me, I struggled everyday without talking to anyone about my emotions.

As I was in the transition process to Alternative Provision I felt nervous as I was going to an unfamiliar place with people I had never met before. The transition over to Alternative Provision was the best decision me and my mam had made. When I first started I wouldn't make eye contact with anyone or speak to anyone. Around 5 months after once I had settled into the environment and got to know everyone I started feeling a lot more comfortable, it was like a weight was released from my shoulders. I soon began to realise my worth, I finally found the place that was right for me. I have struggled all the way from primary school until year 10 when I started Alternative Provision. An Alternative Provision is different to a mainstream school, I had more staff to talk to about my mental health people who weren't teachers'to me that felt like they were patient in dealing with my mental health which helped me get right, then they worked on helping me get my grades.

Figure 9.8 What staff need to know about me

Step 3. Week 2

It was imperative to agree and share the strategies and approaches to support Ned promptly. It was evident from observations of Ned in week 1 that he would benefit from time in nurture provision with consistent staff and a small number of CYP, and support from Lilly, the school therapy dog. As part of his provision, Ned was allocated a key worker, who he chose, who he could confide in if he felt unsettled or needed support. The key worker met informally with Ned daily, and captured and recorded his views on the Child Protection Online Monitoring System (CPOMS) and Behaviour Watch (an online database to record incidents regarding individual students' positive and negative behaviours). A working together plan (Table 9.3) was co-produced with Ned, his caregivers and the key worker, and this was shared with staff alongside the SNAP B profile. Daily feedback (focusing on the positives) was shared with Ned and his caregivers.

Table 9.3 Ned's working together plan

What I find difficult

Having others in my space
Answering questions without being given time to think
Physical contact

Green	
Support strategies	**What Ned will do and say when he is calm and happy**
Let me have time to think about what you are asking me	I will answer questions
	I will look at the teachers
Don't make me look at you	
Don't give me too many instructions at once	• I will follow instructions
Let me leave the classroom two minutes early so I am not in busy or crowded areas where I may get pushed or there may be a risk of physical contact	• I will face you
Remind me when it is my turn to spend time with Lilly	

Amber	
Support strategies	**What Ned will do, say and look like when he is *becoming* anxious and agitated**
Let me take Lilly for a walk around school	• I will turn away from you when you talk to me
Give me the option to see my key worker	• I won't smile or laugh at jokes
	• I won't answer questions
	• I will ask to leave the class or to see Lilly
	• I will fidget in my seat
	• I might throw my work on the floor
• I won't answer questions in class	Ask me to do a task that involves leaving the classroom or gives me the opportunity to go to a quiet space
• I will ask to leave the class or indicate I need to leave by showing you my card	

(Continued)

205

Table 9.3 (Continued) Ned's working together plan

• I won't smile much • I will fidget in my seat • I will throw my work on the floor	Don't ask me to join in group work or to speak in front of the class Let the teachers know I find it difficult to look at them when they are talking to me

Red

Support strategies	What Ned will do when he is in crisis
Don't talk about my family Sit or stand next to me, not opposite me – it makes me feel threatened Offer me some cold water Speak quietly to me	• I will shout • I will get itchy • I will crack my fingers • I might ask for space • I might hit or try to fight other children • I will not be able to listen to teachers • I won't be able to control my reactions if someone touches me

Blue

Support strategies	What Ned does, says and looks like to tell us he is calming down
Help me return to green in about 15 minutes Give me choices to make things right Take me away from the rest of the class	• I will begin to look at you • I may say sorry • I will stop shouting or speak more quietly • I will stroke Lilly

Adapted from The Challenging Behaviour Foundation (2021)

Step 4. Month 1

A review with Ned and his caregivers to discuss the effectiveness of the home and school interventions and strategies. The review included an opportunity for Ned and his caregivers to share positive changes or concerns they may have. The positive outcome identified were as follows:

- Positive relationship developed with his key worker, Lilly and other staff members
- Ability to work alongside other CYP in some group activities
- Reduction in negative incidents/safeguarding referrals
- Improvement of attendance
- Enthusiasm for work-related learning and work experience

- Positive feedback from his caregivers, going to bed on time, completing chores and following most instructions

Step 5. Term 1 (to be repeated termly)

A re-assessment was carried out using the same SNAP B questionnaires. The profiles from the start of his placement and termly versions were compared, with progress shared and celebrated. Ned was encouraged to share his views, wishes and feelings of the impact of his school exclusion by writing a letter to the referring school.

Chapter summary

- Ensuring the CYP and their caregivers contribute their opinions is key to developing trust with a school.
- The initial admission meeting is an invaluable opportunity to unpick past behaviours and establish an insight into the family dynamic.
- Tone of voice, body language and, most importantly, a smile goes a long way in supporting transition to a new school.
- Collaborative approaches are needed to support transition periods, not only as the child starts a new school but also as the child goes through smaller transitions during the day.
- Regularly collecting the views of CYP, caregivers and staff supports the effectiveness of provision and practice.

 Further reading

Feiler, A. (2010) *Engaging 'Hard to reach' parents: Teacher – parent collaboration to promote children's learning.* New Jersey: Wiley.

Lendrum, A., Barlow, A. and Humphrey, N. (2015) 'Developing positive school – home relationships through structured conversations with parents of learners with special educational needs and disabilities (SEND)', *Jorsen*, 15(2), pp. 87–96.

Martin-Denham, S. and Watts, S. (2019) *SENCO handbook: Leading provision and practice*. London: SAGE Publications, Ltd.

Nemeth, K., Ramsey, K. and Derry, K. (2019) *Families & educators together: Building great relationships that support young children.*

References

DfE (2020) *Permanent and fixed-period exclusions in England*. Available at: https://explore-education-statistics.service.gov.uk/find-statistics/permanent-and-fixed-period-exclusions-in-england (Accessed: 8 February 2021).

DfE (2021) *Schools, pupils and their characteristics*. Available at: https://explore-education-statistics.service.gov.uk/find-statistics/school-pupils-and-their-characteristics

Hodder Education (2019) *SNAP – special needs assessment profile*. Available at: https://snap.rsassessment.com/#/core/welcome (Accessed: 9 December 2021).

Hutchinson, J. and Crenna-Jennings, W. (2019) *Unexplained pupil exits from schools: Further analysis and data by multi-academy trust and local authority*. London: Education Policy Institute.

IntegratED (2020) *Fewer exclusions. Better alternative provision – IntegratED Annual Report 2020*. London: Porticus.

Martin-Denham, S. (2020) *The enablers and barriers to successful managed moves: The voice of children, caregivers and professionals*. Sunderland: University of Sunderland.

Martin-Denham, S. and Donaghue, J. (2020) *Out of sight, out of mind? Managed moves in England*. Sunderland: University of Sunderland. Available at: https://sure.sunderland.ac.uk/id/eprint/11883/.

Parentkind (2018) *School exclusion: Parents share their experiences and views. A response to the Education Select Committee and*

Government Consultation on the disproportionately high levels of Special Educational Needs and Disabilities (SEND) pupils affected by exclusion. Kent: Parentkind.

The Challenging Behaviour Foundation (2021) *Resource – Positive behaviour support planning: Part 3.* Available at: https://www. challengingbehaviour.org.uk/understanding-challenging-behaviour/ what-is-challenging-behaviour/resource-positive-behaviour-support-planning-part-3/ (Accessed: 5 December 2021).

Waite, P., Patalay, P., Moltrecht, B., McElroy, E. and Creswell, C. (2020) *Covid-19 worries, parent/carer stress and support needs, by child special educational needs and parent/carer work status. 2.* Oxford: Oxford University.

10 | Co-producing SMART targets for children with social, emotional and mental health needs

Johanna Butler

The chapter outlines two CPD sessions. In our provision, we have timetabled weekly CPD on a Wednesday afternoon. Each session is up to one and a half hours long. The first session included six parts, a mixture of activities and information sharing, each lasting between 10 and 15 minutes. The second session had two parts, as a large amount of time was given to discussion of experiences during part 1.

About Hopespring

Hopespring is a charity that operates independent therapeutic schools for CYP aged 11–16 who have been permanently excluded from at least one school or have not attended school for extended periods. Our primary focus is supporting children with SEMH needs. By the nature of the provision, it can be assumed all our learners have special educational needs and/or disabilities (SEND), whether these are formally recognised or not. The staff team is made up of a multidisciplinary group, including qualified teachers, therapeutically trained counsellors, dual-role teacher-therapists, a speech and language therapist, a consultant child and adolescent psychiatrist, and experienced support staff. All staff are a key worker for at least one young person – as such, they liaise with their home and collaborate in writing shared targets. This chapter explores how to make SMART targets person-centred for secondary school–age learners with SEMH needs.

                    DOI: 10.4324/9781003261506-11

It also shares how we used continuous professional development (CPD) to develop how we co-produced targets with CYP and their caregivers.

CPD session 1a. Warm-up

Prior to beginning the session, the first task was to create a space where participants could be transparent about their thoughts, feelings and attitudes coming into the training. Negative experiences become thoughts that stop participants from fully engaging (Blocksidge, 2021). Addressing these and reshaping these thoughts together allow participants to engage more fully with the process. For example, a participant enters training negatively with this thought:

> I hate target setting. It's so meaningless.

When this is raised in the group, it can be addressed. Acknowledging why it is meaningless (e.g., it's not SMART) helps challenge the closed assumption. An open thought might instead be this:

> Maybe if we did SMART targets with children, it would make them more meaningful. I will see whether this has been the cause of my negative experiences in the past.

CPD session 1b. Jargon busting

Once the negative thoughts had been shared and reframed, teaching on jargon busting and understanding the legal responsibilities of schools helped set the scene and purpose of SMART target setting. During the training, it was made explicit that all schools have a statutory obligation to ensure that young people with SEND are supported by a curriculum that helps build their cultural capital and meets their needs (Ofsted, 2021).

The focus of the session was to explain jargon, legislation, regulations and acronyms (Table 10.1) around target setting, particularly within SEND (including Hopespring-specific terminology). While some members of the team are familiar with specialist terminology, previous experience varies.

Jargon creeps into our areas of specialism and can vary across disciplines. For example, speech and language therapy can be SLT or SALT.

Table 10.1 Jargon busting and SEND regulations (for an extensive list, see Glossary of terms)

Acronym	Definition
AfL	Assessment for Learning
EHCP	education, health and care plan
IEP	individual education plan
ILP	individual learning plan
PEP	Personal Education Plan
SEND	Special educational needs and disabilities
SLT	Senior Leadership Team
SALT	speech and language therapy
SENCO	special educational needs coordinator
SMART	specific, measurable, achievable, relevant, and timed
Legislation/Convention	**Summary**
CAFA 2014	Makes provision about children, families and people with special educational needs or disabilities; to make provision about the right to request flexible working; and for connected purposes.
Equality Act 2010	Legally protects people from discrimination in the workplace and in wider society.
UN Convention on the Rights of the Child (UNCRC) 1989	The Convention has 54 articles that cover all aspects of a child's life and sets out the civil, political, economic, social and cultural rights that all children everywhere are entitled to. It also explains how adults and governments must work together to make sure all children can enjoy all their rights.
Regulation	**Summary**
SEND code of practice (DfE and DoH, 2015)	The code provides guidance and practical advice to local authorities, schools, early education settings and others on how to carry out their duties under the CAFA (2014).
Education Inspection Framework (Ofsted, 2019)	Sets out how Ofsted inspects education settings registered in England.

Both can be confusing; in education, SLT can refer to the Senior Leadership Team, and some staff and students know that salt is what you put on chips.

In addition, introducing staff to the legal responsibility for person-centred and SMART target setting can help expand the purpose of training. The SEND code of practice states this:

LAs must have regard to the views, wishes and feelings of the child, child's parent or young person, their aspirations, the outcomes they wish to seek and the support they need to achieve them.

(DfE and DoH, 2015, 9.12)

It also suggests this:

an EHC outcome should be personal and not expressed from a service perspective; it should be something that those involved should have control and influence over . . . and should be specific, measurable, achievable, realistic and timed.

(9.66)

CPD session 1c. Bloom's taxonomy of affective processes

The purpose of this CPD session was 'to discuss and review Bloom's taxonomy of affective Processes' (Krathwohl, Bloom and Masia, 1973). Bloom created several taxonomies, and while his taxonomy of cognitive processes (Chapter 1) is commonly used. We find Bloom's taxonomy of Affective Processes most useful for measuring improvement within our setting (Table 10.2). While academic progress is valued, many of our young people have been disengaged from education before attending Hopespring, and therefore, we create targets that measure engagement.

CPD session 1d. Reflective activity – Getting it wrong

The aim of part 1d is to consolidate the activities and learning from parts 1a to 1c. For this session, I used the example of a year 11 young person called Mack. He had an EHCP, and his primary need was categorised as SEMH.

At Hopespring, we adapted the passport subcategories (Figure 10.1) found in Martin-Denham and Watts (2019) and created a one-page

213

Table 10.2 Bloom's taxonomy of affective categories

Affective process	SMART targets: common verbs
Receiving phenomena: Awareness, willingness to hear and selected attention.	Asks, chooses, describes, follows, gives, holds, identifies, locates, names, points to, selects, sits, erects, replies and uses
Responding to phenomena: Active participation on the part of the learners. Attends and reacts to a particular phenomenon. Learning outcomes may emphasise compliance in responding, willingness to respond, or satisfaction in responding (motivation).	Answers, assists, aids, complies, conforms, discusses, greets, helps, labels, performs, practises, presents, reads, recites, reports, selects, tells and writes
Valuing: The worth or value a person attaches to a particular object, phenomenon or behaviour. This ranges from simple acceptance to a more complex state of commitment. Valuing is based on the internalisation of a set of specified values, while clues to these values are expressed in the learner's overt behaviour and are often identifiable.	Completes, demonstrates, differentiates, explains, follows, forms, initiates, invites, joins, justifies, proposes, reads, reports, selects, shares, studies and works
Organisation: Organises values into priorities by contrasting different values, resolving conflicts and creating a unique value system. The emphasis is on comparing, relating and synthesising values.	Adheres, alters, arranges, combines, compares, completes, defends, explains, formulates, generalises, identifies, integrates, modifies, orders, organises, prepares, relates and synthesises
Internalising values (characterisation): Has a value system that controls their behaviour. The behaviour is pervasive, consistent, predictable and most importantly, characteristic of the learner. Instructional objectives are concerned with the student's general adjustment patterns (personal, social, emotional).	Acts, discriminates, displays, influences, listens, modifies, performs, practises, proposes, qualifies, questions, revises, serves, solves and verifies

Krathwohl, Bloom and Masia (1973)

document termed in our provision as an individual learning plan (ILP). This is used in conjunction with the EHCP or SEN support plan to maintain a regular and person-centred focus. The targets should reflect the EHCP or

- A photograph of the child
- Information about the child (I would like you to know that)
- How they learn (I learn best when I can)
- What they find hard (I find it difficult to/when)
- What supports them (It would help me if)
- How they help themselves (I will do this if)
- It should also give the name of their key worker, form tutor, pastoral contact and any access arrangements and external support they are currently receiving

Figure 10.1 Passport subcategories
(Martin-Denham and Watts, 2019)

SEN support plan, give smaller bite-size targets to focus on weekly and give our learners the best opportunity to meet their end of key stage outcomes (see Figures 10.2, 10.3 and 10.4 for examples). Through using ILPs, we hope to increase a young person's awareness of their strengths and needs so that in adulthood, they will be able to self-advocate for their strengths and reasonable adjustments that may be required.

Using this one-page format does not work for everyone. Some of our learners would not be able to manage all the information. In these cases, the ILP can be used as a framework to record learners' views, which are gleaned through everyday relationship activities, conversations and support. Learners will often talk about their targets, strengths and needs in an unpressured and un-orchestrated situation. The skill for staff is to capture these views and document them in a meaningful way for a student. However, Mack was an articulate young person who could visually and aurally process the ILP format.

I used my experience co-producing Mack's ILP in training to demonstrate how easily we can think we are being SMART and person-centred but miss the mark. I had written an ILP for Mack based on what I knew about him. Then during a target setting lesson, he was given a blank ILP framework to fill in. Mack filled his in (see Figure 10.2) and highlighted what he felt were his strengths and needs.

After the lesson, I compared the ILP I had drafted to his draft. I thought that the themes were similar, so I showed him the one I had written. I asked what he thought and was surprised when he responded, 'I don't see myself in this at all'. See Figure 10.3 for the ILP I showed Mack.

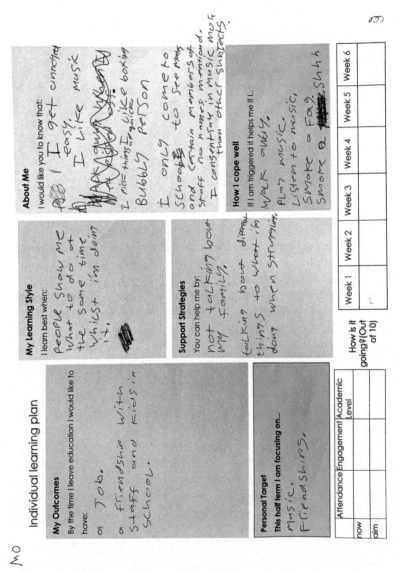

Figure 10.2 The ILP form that Mack completed based on his views

Mack's Individual learning plan

My Outcomes

By the time I leave education I would like to have:

- Healthy strategies to manage stress and negative emotions, as evidenced by being able to quit smoking cannabis and cigarettes
- continued to develop skills that will help me succeed when I live independently including time and money management
- Relevant qualifications to equip me for the working world

Personal Target

This half term I am focusing on...

- **Developing an arsenal of healthy alternatives to managing stress and anxiety**

My Learning Style

I learn best when I:

- Am not anxious about life outside of school
- Know exactly what I am doing and have been given direct instructions
- Have space to myself where I am not distracted by others
- Know that my work is valued

Support Strategies

You can help me by:

- Putting your hand on my shoulder and helping me see that I am in distress
- Give me an option out, such as music
- Verbally encouraging me about what I am good at
- Taking time to listen to what I am finding hard

About Me

I would like you to know that:

- I love music, its my passion, the place I can explore my feelings, and where I feel most at home.
- I am great at learning, I sometimes find it difficult to focus or know why I am learning.
- I am driven to do well in life and want to make something of myself.
- I like to be funny, and will be rude about myself before anyone else is.
- I am a loyal friend, and find it hard when friendships fade.
- I can be loud and seem aggressive or over excited. When I go to far it annoys me and others.

How I cope well

If I am triggered it helps me if I...

- Play music
- Talk to a trusted adult

I don't see myself at all in this

Week 6

	Attendance
now	
aim	

Figure 10.3 Screenshot of initial ILP, which Mack did not feel reflected his voice

217

I told the staff at training that in response to this feedback, I took some time to reflect on what had gone wrong. I asked the following:

What mattered to Mack?

It was clear that his focus was friendships. In Figure 10.2, you can see that I suggested social relationships affect his behaviour, but I had not framed it from Mack's voice. I had framed it from a service perspective. The language I had used meant that Mack could not see himself in what he read. It was in the first person but not in Mack's voice. This led us as a team to reflect on what might be happening here:

- Who was this ILP document really for?
- Who was it going to help?
- Had it become a box-ticking exercise or something to show Ofsted or something else?

Whatever it was, it had completely missed its meaning for Mack, and it was not something he felt he controlled or had influence over. It was not achievable or relevant for him. This led to a revised ILP based on what Mack said, and this framed specific, measurable, achievable, relevant and timed targets around Mack's desired outcomes. See Figure 10.4.

CPD session 1e. Reflection

Following the case study example of Mack in CPD session 1d, staff were invited to reflect on the learners they were key worker for, to consider the following:

- How do you know that the views are the young person's and are not just service perspectives in the first person?
- What could you do to keep the voice of a young person in SMART targets and documentation?
- Are the targets specific, measurable, achievable, relevant and timed?

M's Individual Learning Plan

hopespring
Therapeutic Learning Provision

My outcomes
By the time I leave education I would like to have:

- Kept friendships with others at school.

- Kept working on cooking and managing money to help me be ready to live on my own.

- Relevant qualifications to equip me for a job. At Hopespring this will be measured by getting Functional Skills (Level 2) and GCSE qualifications (grade 4).

Personal Target
This half term I am focusing on....

- Learning 2 new pieces of music on drums and piano, and writing 2 new songs.

- Keeping friendships, through fixing misunderstandings and failings out after arguements.

- Working towards Level 1 Functional Skills in Maths and English.

My Learning Style
I learn best when:

- People show me what to do at the same time whilst I am doing it.

- I know what the point is in the work I am doing and why it is important for my life.

- I have dealt with anything happening outside of school.

Support Strategies
You can help me by:

- Talking about different things to what I'm doing when struggling.

- Give me an option out, such as music.

- Verbally encouraging me about what I am good at.

- Taking time to listen to what I am finding hard.

About Me
I would like you to know that:

- I get annoyed easily.

- I like music. It helps me stay calm when I freestyle and play music.

- I pick things up quickly.

- I like seeing friends and staff at school.

- I concentrate on music more than anything else.

- I am a bubbly person. I can be loud.

- I like boxing.

How I cope well
If I am triggered it helps me if...

- I can play music.

- I can walk away.

- I can talk to a trusted adult.

- I can smoke.

Figure 10.4 Agreed ILP based on Mack's perception and staff observations

- What is going well with the SMART targets?
- How can the targets be improved while also keeping them person-centred and SMART?

> **Task**
> Start with one target and transform it into a SMART, person-centred target; then describe the support provided to achieve it.

CPD session 1f. Gathering learner voice

The final part of the CPD session was a quickfire ten-minute activity to equip the team for their homework. Gathering student and parent voices is vital for ensuring that targets remain person-centred and SMART, but there are lots of creative ways in which we can do this.

> **Task**
> Produce a list of 20 ideas to capture student's views. Choose your best three and share them with the group.

While this task might seem unachievable, it pushes participants to think beyond their normal realm of possibility. Table 10.3 shows the final list from our CPD.

> **Homework**
> As part of your key worker role, put these ideas into practice and gather learner voice to be able to create and update the ILPs.

CPD session 2

Three weeks later, the same group of staff gathered on videoconferencing for the second session in our regular weekly CPD slot. Staff had been

Table 10.3 Suggested ways to capture learner voice

Using the school environment/ curriculum	Adapting documentation/meetings
Creating space for conversation when learners are doing another activity; for example, during breaks or during incidental conversations.	Breaking down ILPs, one-page profiles or EHCP to focus on one section at a time (all about me or what others like about me)
Providing a camera and asking them to take a picture of their favourite place in school to understand their preferred place to regulate or feel safe, giving insight into what is important to them. It may also give insight into the targets they want to achieve; for example, a photo of the kitchen showing they enjoy or would like to develop cooking skills.	Staff writing targets based on knowledge and insight of what drives a student and then sharing this with them; for example, if you know that a lot of their behaviour results from wanting to be accepted by peers, write something that reflects this desire (taken from real-life example): *This half term, I am focusing on being a good friend. I am doing this through talking to staff when I feel [learner-given word to describe emotion (e.g., out of control)]. I will know I am achieving this because I will have a whole week where I have [learner provided measure (e.g., not been rude about my friend's appearance)].*
Engaging in target setting around a topic they are interested in; for example, looking at future careers in lessons and sharing ideas on what they need to do to achieve their aspirations.	Sitting with learners and the blank ILP document so they can share their ideas, and if they request it, we can write them together. Have a range of manipulatives and art media available for those who prefer to draw their preferences.
Using pictures to support verbal communication; for example, a young person drawing their future or their feelings on a good day at school.	Focusing on the purpose; for example, some students have multiple meetings across the year (especially if they are cared for). Being able to be supported to take ownership of their meetings and become an active part of them, regardless of their cognitive level. Co-chairing meetings, choosing who is there and changing certain elements of the meetings to make it theirs (e.g., music, seating plans and snacks).
Resources available for visual support; for example, printed adjectives or images of positive qualities for sorting into categories (me or not me).	Split the EHCP into individual sentences and ask the child to choose whether they do something 'all the time', 'sometimes', 'occasionally' or 'never', with the statements that make up the EHCP or support plan and so forth; for example, 'I am considerate of other people' and 'I need people to repeat what they have said'.

reminded the week before about the homework from CPD session 1f – gathering learner voice.

CPD session 2a. How did the homework go?

Using the ideas generated in the last session, staff were asked to give feedback about their experiences of capturing voice. Their reflections were collected on an interactive virtual board and can be seen in Figure 10.5. Although there were some positive experiences, key themes were raised around the barriers to gathering learners' voices:

- Not been attending school
- Disinterested in engaging with the task
- Learners being paranoid about the form and not wanting to be special needs
- Low literacy and cognitive skills not being able to access the ILP

Acknowledging these key themes, training could then be directed in a focused way to help upskill staff, through discussion of barriers and strategies to overcome them. Some barriers were harder to overcome. For example, there is no way to capture a student's voice if you have not had contact with them (i.e., when they have low attendance). However, other barriers using creative thinking were possible to overcome. Paranoia and mental health needs, such as anxiety, low motivation and depression, are barriers for learners. In this case, reframing the task can help staff to think flexibly about student voice. Staff at Hopespring are excellent at building relationships with learners, and they know their students very well. Often, they can gather thoughts and feelings about school, their strengths and difficulties, in conversations and unpressured moments. Reminding our staff that these views count and are valid can give them the confidence to document them.

On one occasion, a student did not want staff to ask her questions about anything outside of school. She became defensive when this was attempted; the ILP format felt threatening to her. For the participants, it was important to develop an understanding that the framework is a tool to build on conversations. For the student, examples of what information was being gathered would be helpful. Writing examples, like 'I am a good friend', 'I

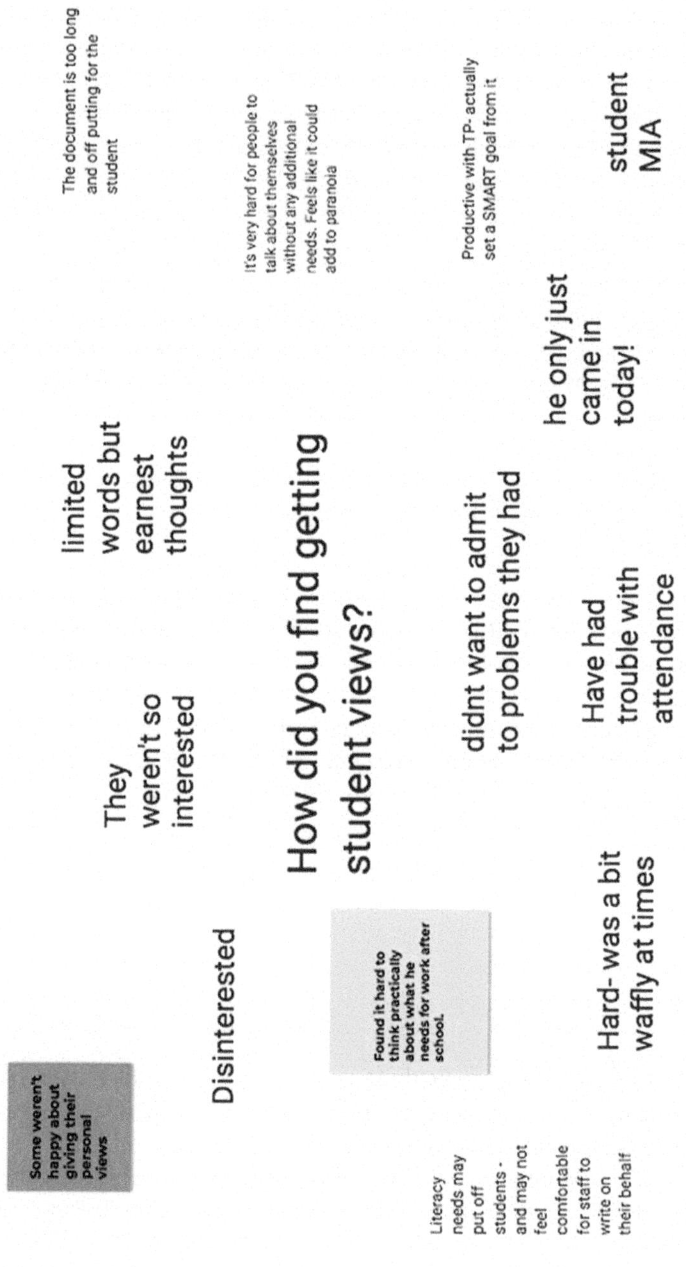

The document is too long and off putting for the student

It's very hard for people to talk about themselves without any additional needs. Feels like it could add to paranoia

Productive with TP- actually set a SMART goal from it

limited words but earnest thoughts

They weren't so interested

student MIA

How did you find getting student views?

he only just came in today!

didnt want to admit to problems they had

Disinterested

Have had trouble with attendance

Found it hard to think practically about what he needs for work after school.

Hard- was a bit waffly at times

Some weren't happy about giving their personal views

Literacy needs may put off students - and may not feel comfortable for staff to write on their behalf

Figure 10.5 Staff feedback on gathering learner voice recorded on virtual interactive board

223

like to meet new people and get to know interesting things about them' or 'I care a lot about people who I know care about me', keep the content positive and help the student imagine what things might be written about. I find that often when a student disengages, becomes defensive or says they 'don't know', it is because they have difficulty generating ideas.

Discussing with the participants at training that we can gather ideas from our students because we know them and have spent time with them helps remove barriers. Instead of the plan or target setting being a rigid form to fill in, they can be a tool to document a student's ideas and views. Where documents are filled in by staff to support idea generation, students still have a choice, but rather than there being infinite options, we help them by making the options finite and giving them a channel into which their own ideas can flow.

CPD session 2b. Making targets SMART

Using the starters in Table 1.4 (Chapter 1), the second activity was to choose one and make it SMART for a student in our care. Participants were reminded of Bloom's taxonomy of verbs for the affective domains (Krathwohl, Bloom and Masia, 1973). Furthermore, they were instructed to take abstract verbs and transform them into concrete action verbs. For example, 'to develop' can be an abstract concept, whereas 'can give examples of' is much more concrete and, therefore, both measurable and achievable. Figure 10.6 demonstrates some of the targets. The sentence framework is adapted from resources on the Thinking for Good app (Expert Apps LTD, 2020).

Chapter summary

- SMART target setting can be difficult, especially for children with SEMH
- Focus is on what is achievable and relevant for the young person, and where appropriate, their families
- Bloom's taxonomy of Affective Processes (Krathwohl, Bloom and Masia, 1973) provides a range of additional verbs when targets are not

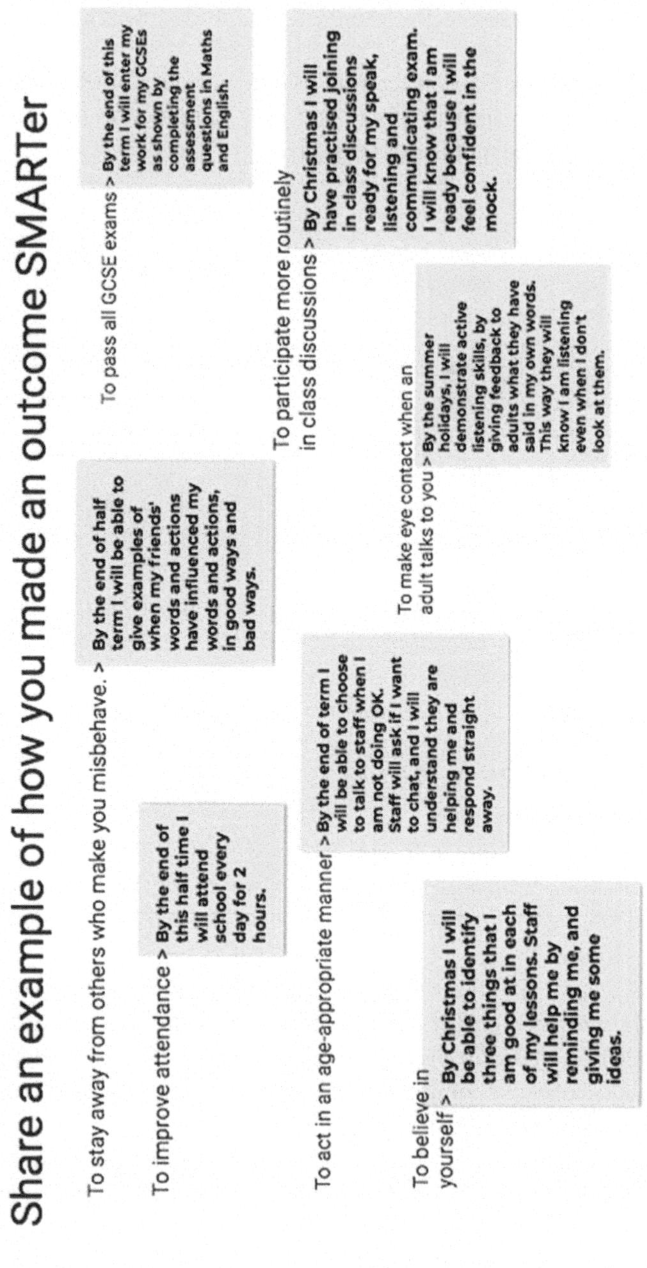

Share an example of how you made an outcome SMARTer

To stay away from others who make you misbehave. > By the end of half term I will be able to give examples of when my friends' words and actions have influenced my words and actions, in good ways and bad ways.

To improve attendance > By the end of this half time I will attend school every day for 2 hours.

To pass all GCSE exams > By the end of this term I will enter my work for my GCSEs as shown by completing the assessment questions in Maths and English.

To participate more routinely in class discussions > By Christmas I will have practised joining in class discussions ready for my speak, listening and communicating exam. I will know that I am ready because I will feel confident in the mock.

To act in an age-appropriate manner > By the end of term I will be able to choose to talk to staff when I am not doing OK. Staff will ask if I want to chat, and I will understand they are helping me and respond straight away.

To make eye contact when an adult talks to you > By the summer holidays, I will demonstrate active listening skills, by giving feedback to adults what they have said in my own words. This way they will know I am listening even when I don't look at them.

To believe in yourself > By Christmas I will be able to identify three things that I am good at in each of my lessons. Staff will help me by reminding me, and giving me some ideas.

Figure 10.6 Examples of transforming towards SMART targets

about academic progress but progress in attitude towards learning or engagement

* Training can support a staff team in thinking about SMART target setting for young people with SEMH and how to reflect on how to overcome barriers to doing this successfully

References

Blocksidge, J. (2021) *What has the greatest impact on organisational performance?* Available at: https://gomadthinking.com/insights/what-has-the-greatest-impact-on-organisational-performance/ (Accessed: 30 November 2021).

Children and Families Act (CAFA) 2014. Available at: https://www.legislation.gov.uk/ukpga/2014/6/contents/enacted (Accessed: 25 November 2021).

Department for Education (DfE) and Department of Health (DoH) (2015) *Special educational needs and disability code of practice: 0 to 25 years.* London: DfE.

Equality Act 2010, c. 15. Available at: http://www.legislation.gov.uk/ukpga/2010/15/contents (Accessed: 7 May 2020).

Expert Apps LTD (2020) *Thinking for good (1.0.10)* [mobile app] (Accessed: 30 November 2021)

Krathwohl, D.R., Bloom, B.S. and Masia, B.B. (1973) *Taxonomy of educational objectives. The classification of educational goals. Handbook II: Affective domain.* New York: David McKay Company Incorporated.

Martin-Denham, S. and Watts, S. (2019) *The SENCO handbook: Leading provision and practice.* London: SAGE Publications, Ltd.

Ofsted (2019) *Education inspection framework.* Available at: https://www.gov.uk/government/publications/education-inspection-framework. (Accessed: 9 March 2022).

Ofsted (2021) *Guidance: School inspection handbook.* Available at: https://www.gov.uk/government/publications/school-inspection-handbook-eif/school-inspection-handbook (Accessed: 3 December 2021).

UNICEF (1989) *The United Nations Convention on the Rights of the Child.* London: UNICEF.

11 | Moving from non-SMART towards SMART targets in a mainstream secondary school

Danny Kilkenny

This chapter describes how a large secondary school changed their approach to target setting. It outlines the processes of leading a self-evaluation and identifying the critical issues in provision and practice for children with SEND. The SENCO and Senior Leadership Team worked with colleagues across the school to implement a series of reviews and provided a range of professional development opportunities to improve the target setting process.

Identifying the critical issues

Before we began planning how to use SMART targets more effectively in SEN support plans, a systematic self-evaluation of the targets being set by both teaching and support staff across the school was undertaken. One of the main findings of the self-evaluation was that neither staff nor parents felt that the targets being set by the wider school, or by the SEN department, for our learners with SEND were appropriate. Table 11.1 shows an SEN support plan from this period illustrating a range of issues. The target 'to make best possible progress towards positive outcomes' reflected more the needs of the school to ensure positive progress figures. It did not reflect the views, wishes or feelings of the CYP or their caregivers. Nor did it actually set a target that was realistic or manageable. As Figure 11.1 illustrates how ill-considered

DOI: 10.4324/9781003261506-12

Table 11.1 A non-SMART SEN support plan

Desired outcome and steps towards meeting it	Intervention/support	Who will carry out this support?	How often will this happen?	How will this be monitored and when?
To make best possible progress towards positive outcomes in year 10, overcoming barriers to his learning caused by his moderate learning difficulty	Quality first teaching Seating planning Class size and support of 1:25	Class teacher	Daily	Class teacher, daily
	Extra time or reader in class and exams	SENCO	During exams	SENCO, annually
	Differentiated classwork and homework Short frequent instructions	Class teacher	Daily	Class teacher, daily
	Ongoing staff training	SENCO	Termly	SENCO, termly
	Encouragement to check personal hygiene	Pastoral support	As needed	Pastoral support, termly
To make best possible progress towards positive outcomes in Yr 10 overcoming barriers to his learning caused by his moderate learning difficulty.	Access when needed to first aid, toilet and hygiene room facilities	SENCO and learning support assistant (LSA)	As needed	SENCO, termly

targets can cause children and young people (CYP) to feel disengaged from learning. Other issues included the following:

- The desired outcomes are neither measurable nor observable
- The interventions/support do not relate to the desired outcome
- The interventions/support include irrelevant information (quality first teaching (QTF) is universal) and should not be on an SEN support plan, neither should staff training

Alongside a review of how we set targets as a school, we also decided that a wider self-evaluation of the SEN department was needed (Table 11.2). This involved the Senior Leadership Team (SLT), the SENCO, LSAs, higher

Figure 11.1 Disengaged young person

Table 11.2 Example of SEN review proforma

Leadership and management SEN review

Theme	Requirement	Comment	Actions needed	RAG	Review date
Family engagement in a positive way that supports a CYP's education	Ofsted (2019) Framework	Some parental involvement but not consistent and not evaluated enough	**Action:** Must look at implementation of a consistent person-centred approach		February 2021
High ambition for all CYP		Moving to mixed prior attainment classes has raised ambition; curriculum on offer is ambitious for all	**N/A**		February 2021

Theme	Requirement	Comment	Actions needed	RAG	Review date
Identification of SEND needs is a focus		One-page profiles can be sometimes too generic, but identification of need does take place	**Action:** Support plans need to be more individualised; specific outcomes based on need and barriers to learning need to be addressed		February 2021
Strategies to meet SEND needs are effective and visible		Strategies are in place but are too generic and not monitored against measurable outcomes	**Action:** A review of all strategies and targets as well as the monitoring of impact needs to be implemented		February 2021

level teaching assistants (HLTA) and a sample of caregivers and CYP, and included a red, amber and green flagged response.

As shown from the self-evaluation, the review highlighted to SLT that the current strategies and targets we had in place to support learners were too vague. This provided a clear rationale for change.

REFLECTIVE ACTIVITY

Have you got a clear knowledge and understanding of what the development need or issues are in your context? Do you have evidence to support your claim? How would you articulate the issues and solutions to members of your Senior Leadership Team or other colleagues in school?

Follow-up consultation

Another area highlighted as red in our self-evaluation was engagement with caregivers. As a large secondary school, the SEN team found it difficult to engage meaningfully. The leadership team made a conscious decision that we wanted their views to feed into any targets set for CYP. As such, using our school social media and education platforms, we sent out an electronic survey (Figure 11.2).

Figure 11.2 Using social media to capture caregiver's views

Key questions asked on the survey included the following:

1   Have you seen your child's SEN support plan targets?
2   Were you involved in the process of setting your child's targets? If not, do you know how the targets were generated?
3   What kind of targets would you like to see set for your child?
4   How would you like to be involved in the process? How often?
5   What are your wishes and feelings about what your child needs?

Their responses included the following:

- 'I know that 'John' has had targets set, but I haven't seen them and I wasn't involved. I presume the targets probably came from the primary school teachers'.
- 'It is important for me that 'James' does well at school academically. I want him to get good grades but I think he also needs targets to help him be happy, like make friends'.

• 'I haven't really seen any specific targets around her SEN needs. I have seen targets from her subject teachers though, when we get reports home and at parents evenings'.

The consultation confirmed what our self-evaluation raised, that current SEN support plan targets were not created in consultation with caregivers nor CYP. Nor were they reflective of the wider holistic needs of the individual. In many cases, targets were still being set at the latter stages of key stages 3 and 4, based on information from discussions with primary school teachers in preparation for transition to secondary school.

Creating a whole-school shared vision

Having established that as a school we needed to change our approach to SEN support plan targets, the next step for the SLT was to ensure all teaching and support staff understood why changes needed to be made. In our minds, it was clear that targets were not specific, measurable, achievable, relevant or time-bound (SMART), nor developed in conjunction with caregivers or CYP. What was important was that the staff understood how this was demotivating learners and making the provision they were receiving in the classroom less effective as shown in Figure 11.3.

Figure 11.3 De-motivated young person in school

Our vision was for all SEN support targets to be SMART and co-produced. To support staff buy-in for this vision, we gathered evidence (Table 11.3) from a number of sources that we could use as a basis for discussion. We wanted staff to see the current target setting process so that they could understand the issue for themselves.

Evidence 1: learner voice

My targets are to achieve Level 4s in all of my subjects. But I know I am struggling with my reading and I can't really do English at all so how am I even supposed to get that.

I know that my target is to make sure I am doing well in all my subjects and make sure that I don't get distracted in class. So, that means I have to concentrate more.

As can be seen in these snapshots, there were a number of critical issues. These included the following:

- Lack of CYP and caregiver voice
- Lack of specific focus about the CYP or on their needs
- No clear identification of reasonable adjustments
- Reference to quality first teaching (QFT), which is universally provided
- Targets being set that were unrealistic and demotivating

Table 11.3 Evidence 2: one-page profile

Name	Range
Learning needs	**Exam concessions**
Cognition and learning	Reader
Low across the board	Up to 25% extra time
Pastoral support and concessions	**Historic information**
Year manager and SEN team	Primary school spent a lot of time with support staff
support where needed	Lots of one-to-one support and reading intervention
Teaching and learning support	**Learner voice**
and concessions	Wants to do well; interested in music and sport
Quality first teaching	Sometimes finds work difficult and challenging
Differentiated class and homework	

The SLT knew that making changes to SMART targets would benefit CYP as well as give caregivers a more active role in their child's education. However, we needed to consider where this change in approach would sit among other whole-school initiatives in curriculum development and feedback approaches being launched at the time. Changing the way we approached discussing and setting targets for our learners with SEN was going to impact on staff workload. For teaching staff to be on board with the changes senior leaders were proposing, it was important that they had a shared vision. It was important for the SLT to take the time to consider whether the SENCO and the team around them had the time and the resources to embed and sustain the changes that we were seeking to bring about (Educational Endowment Fund (EEF), 2019a). Over the past few years, it was felt that the responsibility for learners with SEN had been moved more and more to solely sit with the SENCO as illustrated in Figure 11.4.

Figure 11.4 Overworked SENCO

The Education Endowment Fund (EEF), in their 'schools guide to implementation' (2019a), highlight the importance of treating the implementation of any new idea as a process, not an event. One of the early stages of their implementation process is ensuring that you identify a clear area of improvement. It was important to the school that before we shared with staff any ideas about what we were going to change or implement, we had a clear understanding and vision of what we hoped to achieve based on evidence. The EEF Implementation Template (2019b) provides a useful reflective activity for leaders to consider.

 REFLECTIVE ACTIVITY

Using the EEF (2019b) template (Figure 11.5), reflect on the current interventions in your setting.

- What is the problem?
- What needs to change?
- How will you make changes?
- What would be the benefits of making changes?
- Have you or your team got the time to implement, embed and sustain the change you are considering?

Leading a series of CPD

At this early planning stage, it was important to speak to the SLT in charge of professional development to ensure that we were given the time to provide training on SMART targets. We felt that our staff would benefit from some additional understanding of their role within the SEN team. A series of professional development sessions over a half-term led up to the SMART target training that was designed to increase the classroom teachers' understanding of their role in supporting learners with SEN.

There are over 60 classroom teachers in the school, with 8 support staff (HLTAs/LSAs) with a range of experience and qualifications.

PITTING EVIDENCE TO WORK: A SCHOOL'S GUIDE TO IMPLEMENTATION

Implementation plan template

Education
Endowment
Foundation

Problem (why?)	Intervention Description (what?)	Implementation Activities (how?)	Implementation Outcomes (how well?)	Final Outcomes (and so?)
What needs to change e.g. teacher behaviour, student behaviour, attainment?	What are the essential 'active ingredients' of the intervention? What activities and behaviours will you see when it is working?	How will it be done? What blend of activities are required?	How will you know that it is working? Do staff feel the approach is feasible and useful? **Short term**	How will pupils, teachers and the school benefit?
			Medium term	
			Long term	

Figure 11.5 Implementation plan template

EEF (2019a)

REFLECTIVE ACTIVITY

Do you need to plan other aspects of CPD before your main CPD to encourage staff buy-in?

Do you need to think about creating a shared vision of why this is important?

If staff are going to be asked to do more, how have you ensured they see its value?

The five CPD sessions

The following section outlines the five CPD sessions. The school provides 1-hour 50-minute slots weekly for professional development. Typically, the five sessions took around 50 minutes with the staff working together. They then split into departments to discuss how they would respond to the ideas they had been presented with in their own contexts.

Session 1: capturing child and caregiver voice

Objectives

- To identify current approaches used to capture child and caregiver voice (Figure 11.6)
- To understand the SEND code of practice (DfE and DoH, 2015) position on the role of the child and caregiver
- To establish a consistent and effective approach to gathering child and caregiver voice

Overview of session 1

This session with teaching and support staff was a group discussion. Groups included teaching staff from different departments, with varying experience

Figure 11.6 Capturing child and caregiver voice

and a member of the SLT. This approach was implemented to ensure each group would have a range of views.

The SEN team recorded and used the results of the discussions to plan a new trial approach to gathering child and caregiver voices to inform SEN support plan targets.

The decision we reached was to restructure our support team so that one member of the SEN support team was allocated to each of our five year groups, with one team member assigned as a floater. To facilitate this, each of the SEN support team was taken off the timetable for a week, covered by the floater, to meet with the CYP and their caregivers in their year group, to collect views on what mattered to them. The information was then fed back to classroom teachers.

Session 2: quality first teaching (QFT)

Objectives

- To recognise the key areas that make up QFT in line with the EEF Teaching of SEN Framework (2021)
- To evaluate current practice in line with the QFT framework
- To apply the techniques of QFT in the context of your own classroom (Figure 11.7).

Overview

The teaching and learning lead at the school went through the EEF (2021) QFT model with all teaching staff. Discussions were held about

Figure 11.7 What quality first teaching might include

the reasoning behind each technique, and examples were given of how these techniques could be applied in the classroom. Staff were then sent to departments to look at each section of the framework individually so they could plan, where necessary, a consistent department approach to their delivery. This was followed up with instructional coaching sessions delivered by lead practitioners to further ensure the consistency and quality of delivery. The subsequent template was used to record classroom visits as part of the coaching approach (Table 11.4). These records were only used for discussions in instructional coaching sessions.

Table 11.4 Record of classroom visits

In-class strategies to achieve targets

(A) Quality first teaching

Teachers

(1) Scaffolding

1	Clear instructions and specific/targeted questioning to ensure understanding of tasks
2	Writing frames and success criteria to give guidance when working independently
3	Reinforce (daily) expectations in terms of equipment and effort (scaffolded expectations)
4	Differentiated sheets produced where there is a literacy need
5	Checks after guided practice phase of learning before moving to independence

(2) Direct instruction

1	Teacher-led explanation clear and focused
2	Resources considered (including PowerPoints) to avoid cognitive overload of learner
3	Teacher-led explanation is followed by a clear period of guided practice before independent work

(3) Technology

1	Visualisers, where available, are used to model work to support learner
2	Where necessary, laptop is provided to assist learners' note taking

(4) Cognitive/Metacognitive

1	Teachers should ensure they talk through how they solve problems or take steps
2	Learners should use the metacognitive plan (plan, monitor and evaluate)
3	Work is chunked into sections, with one question at a time, or checklists to support information being processed

Session 3: the role of the class teacher in supporting learners with SEN

Objectives

- To review the SEND code of practice (DfE and DoH, 2015) and identify the role of the classroom teacher in supporting learners with SEN
- To reflect and evaluate on your own current practice in supporting learners with SEN
- To identify changes you can make to your practice to more effectively support learners with SEN

Overview

To start this session, we asked staff to give us their views on who was responsible for SEN across the school. We then asked all teaching staff to read the relevant chapters of the SEND code of practice (DfE and DoH, 2015). We asked them to highlight in the text any references to the role of the teacher. They then used this to construct a list, which the group shared about what a teacher should be doing.

We then asked them independently to review their own practice and to honestly reflect on their own practice and then, in pairs, consider what changes they would make.

Session 4: the graduated approach

Objectives

- To understand and articulate the principles of the graduated approach
- To discuss and review the classroom teachers' role in the graduated approach

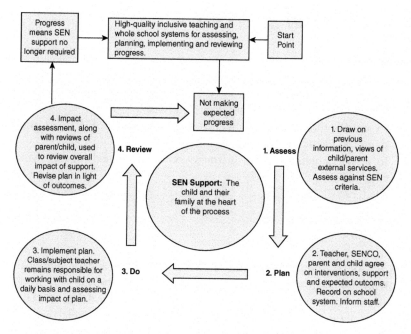

Figure 11.8 The graduated approach

Overview

This session was shorter than the other sessions delivered. We sent out the model of the graduated approach for SEN support in advance of the sessions (Figure 11.8). The SENCO talked through each of the stages (assess, plan, do and review) in turn. Staff could see the links, for example, between sessions delivered on high-quality teaching, and the graduated approach cycle, which emphasised the relevance of what we had been doing. The majority of the session was spent discussing the importance of the planning phase, as our overall aim was to move to developing SMART targets.

Session 5: SMART target CPD

Objectives

- To identify the features of non-SMART or ineffective targets and understand the impact of these targets on learners
- To identify the features of effective targets that are SMART and understand the impact of these targets on learners
- To create targets for three learners you teach, based on the SMART target CPD

Overview

The SMART target training was delivered by the teaching and learning lead who had worked with Sarah Martin-Denham, the NA SENCO Award Programme Leader at the University of Sunderland. The CPD used Bloom's taxonomy of educational objectives to write targets that were SMART (see Chapter 1). Staff were first encouraged to discuss current SEN support targets (Table 11.5) and were guided to explore why they were not SMART.

Table 11.5 Examples of non-SMART targets from SEN support plans

Target number	The target
1	Remain focused during the lesson and attempt all questions given
2	Remain focused during the lesson and attempt all work to the best of your ability
3	Remain focused on the task given without becoming distracted
4	Listen at all times and follow instructions
5	Don't give up when you can't answer questions
6	Try your best, even when you get things wrong

The structure of the activity was as follows, considering the targets in Table 11.5:

- Is each target, 1–6, SMART?
- Could you observe or measure the child's achievement of these targets?
- Would these targets be appropriate for a child?

To help you in your task you may want to consider the following case study:

Case study: Danny

Danny is in year 9. He has a diagnosis of ADHD and is on SEN support. He receives medication every morning from the school nurse for his ADHD but sometimes forgets to take it because he arrives to school late. Danny loves school; his favourite lesson is history. He has a green card that allows him to leave the classroom when he gets frustrated and distracted so he can go and work with an LSA. He uses the card quite frequently, which means he spends a lot of time out of class.

To conclude CPD session 5, the staff were shown how to use the Bloom's taxonomy (as illustrated in Chapter 1) in a template to create SMART targets. To facilitate this task, we provided one-page profiles and encouraged them to think about the training they had received, as set out in this chapter. We then asked them to try and write two SMART targets for a CYP with SEN they taught. Table 11.6 shares a teacher's targets for a CYP named Sarah. Sarah is diagnosed with dyscalculia and, due to this, has low self-esteem, particularly in mathematics.

 REFLECTIVE ACTIVITY

Consider how you would respond to the following questions during CPD on SMART targets:

1   What do I do if a learner is doing well in my subject? Do they still need a target?

2 Some learners are recorded as SEMH, and I can't think of obvious targets?

3 If I don't have a good relationship with a CYP, can someone else ask them their views, wishes and feelings?

4 I am worried about meeting with caregivers, what support can you give me?

5 Who will review the targets? Will we be given time to attend SEN support review meetings?

Table 11.6 Post-CPD training SEN support targets

Target (specific)	Measurable	Achievable	Realistic resource/ provision	Timed
Lower-order thinking skills: remembering				
Sarah will recall three positive things that have happened each day	Sarah will state three good things that have happened. This will be recorded in her feeling good book	Sarah has told her teacher she wants to feel good at something and her mum is supportive	Adult available to support, and feeling good book is in use in class. Mum is keen to read feeling good book with Sarah at home	To be achieved by October half-term 2022
Higher-order thinking skills: evaluate				
Sarah will choose appropriate manipulatives to allow her to estimate answers to real-life problems with addition beyond 20–30	The class teacher will be able to observe the resources Sarah selects and how she solves problems with them	Sarah has the greatest success in problem-solving when she has access to manipulatives and is keen to learn these skills	The classroom has a range of manipulatives freely available on tables; both Sarah and her caregiver are keen to support independent working	Ongoing monitoring until October half-term 2022

Maintaining support for staff

To help ensure we could support staff in writing these targets and to quality assure what was written, we had pre-trained a group of lead practitioners within the school to help support staff or departments who were struggling to write their targets. It was important to reinforce the SMART target training with follow-up support and have clear lines of help available for anyone asking questions. We made sure time was built into subsequent CPD sessions for drop-ins for any staff requiring additional support.

Reviewing the effectiveness of CPD

At the end of the five CPD sessions, we surveyed a sample of staff to ascertain their understanding of their role in supporting CYP designated with SEN support. The results clearly showed that staff were now much more aware of how important their role as a teacher was.

Some of the comments included the following:

> The biggest change in my thinking came after reading the SEND code of practice. I had never read it before and had no real idea of how important the role of the classroom teacher was. I thought it was pretty much all the responsibility of the SENCO.
>
> I think the biggest change for me is understanding how I can set targets to allow learners to slowly work on removing the barriers they have to achieve success in my subject.
>
> Targets that I set before were ones that a learner would look at working towards completing over an academic year. I can see now that for many learners, that deadline is too distant and targets need to be more manageable and incremental.

Moving towards co-production of provision and practice

For us to fundamentally change not only how staff set targets but also how they view their role in the target-setting process, more time was needed for CPD. There needed to be a clear plan to embed co-production of provision and practice with CYP and their caregivers. We wanted to ensure that, moving forward, staff saw the value in taking quality time to co-produce and to ensure targets that were SMART and based on CYP's and their caregivers' views, wishes and feelings. To achieve this, time was set aside to complete further training. We also planned sessions to reflect on how approaches had changed to teaching pedagogy once targets had been written. Best practice was shared so that staff could see the big picture of what target setting looked like across the school. To support the SENCO in monitoring this process, key individuals were appointed to oversee the quality assurance process. In this way, the SMART target training became the first step of a process, not an isolated professional development event that was delivered and then forgotten about.

After completing one full round of SMART target setting by all class teachers, we held a post-mortem review meeting with a selection of staff, CYP and their caregivers. We wanted to establish exactly where we were on our change journey. The anecdotal results of the review brought to light areas of success and areas for further development.

Chapter summary

- Self-evaluation supports schools in establishing areas of development
- It is important that the SLT share the rationale for change with staff to gain their support and enthusiasm for embedding new systems and processes
- Establish if there is capacity within the school and the SEN team to lead and implement change
- When planning CPD sessions, write SMART targets to ensure you have a clear sense of what you want to achieve
- Ensure you revisit and re-evaluate the changes so new practices are embedded and sustained
- SMART targets must be co-produced with CYP and their caregivers to ensure their views, wishes and feelings are taken into account

 Further reading

Blatchford, P., Russell, A. and Webster, R. (2012) *Reassessing the impact of teaching assistants: How research challenges practice and policy.* 1st edn. New York: Routledge.

Boesley, L. and Crane, L. (2018) 'Forget the health and care and just call them education plans': SENCOs' perspectives on education, health and care plans', *Journal of Research in Special Educational Needs*, 18(S1), pp. 36–47.

Cavendish, W. and Connor, D. (2018) 'Towards authentic IEPs and transition plans: Student, parent, and teacher perspectives', *Learning Disability Quarterly*, 41(1), pp. 32–43.

Cheminais, R. (2015) *Rita Cheminais' handbook for SENCOs*. 2nd edn. Los Angeles: SAGE Publications, Ltd.

Cowne, E.A. (2019) *The SENCO handbook: Leading and managing a whole school approach*. 7th edn. New York: Routledge.

Ekins, A. (2015) *The changing face of special educational needs: Impact and implications for SENCOs, teachers and their schools*. 2nd edn. Milton Park, Abingdon, Oxon; New Yok, NY: Routledge.

Fleming, P. (2019) *Successful middle leadership in secondary schools: A practical guide to subject and team effectiveness*. 2nd edn. New York: Routledge.

Florian, L. and Linklater, H. (2010) 'Preparing teachers for inclusive education: Using inclusive pedagogy to enhance teaching and learning for all', *Cambridge Journal of Education*, 40(4), pp. 369–386.

Martin-Denham, S. (2019) *The SENCO handbook: Leading provision and practice*. Thousand Oaks, CA: SAGE Publications, Ltd.

References

Department for Education (DfE) and Department of Health (DoH) (2015) *Special educational needs and disability code of practice: 0 to 25 years*. London: DfE.

Education Endowment Foundation (2019a) *Putting evidence to work. A school's guide to implementation*. Available at: https://educationendowmentfoundation.org.uk/public/files/Publications/

Implementation/EEF_Implementation_Guidance_Report_2019.pdf (Accessed: 21 October 2021).

Education Endowment Foundation (2019b) *Putting evidence to work. A school's guide to implementation. Template.* Available at: https://educationendowmentfoundation.org.uk/public/files/Publications/Implementation/EEF-Implementation-Plan-Template.pdf (Accessed: 27 October 2021).

Education Endowment Foundation (2021) *Special educational needs in mainstream schools. High quality teaching for pupils with SEND.* Available at: https://d2tic4wvo1iusb.cloudfront.net/guidance-reports/send/EEF_High_Quality_Teaching_for_Pupils_with_SEND.pdf (Accessed: 27 October 2021).

Ofsted (2019) *Education inspection framework.* Available at: https://www.gov.uk/government/publications/education-inspection-framework. (Accessed: 9 March 2022).

12 | Co-producing SMART transitions into further education

Peter Monaghan

This chapter focuses on the provision and experiences of learning support staff within the FE and ACL sector in England. The FE and ACL sector is located between the secondary school setting and universities. Terminology within FE and ACL can be confusing and definitions shift. For this chapter, pupils or students will be referred to as 'learners'. The chapter aims to provide some practical support to learning support staff, teachers, leaders and parents within an FE context and, as such, touches on two key aspects: supporting the transition to FE and setting ambitious SMART targets for FE learners with SEN. Successful learner transitions are proven to dramatically increase retention and progression to FE and training and ultimately sustainable employment.

FE generally provides for young people and adults (16 to 60-plus) on a range of general and vocational training, apprenticeships and education programmes, historically aligned to occupational skills. Learners may attend on a full-time or part-time basis, on short training programmes lasting weeks or two to three years. In some organisations, learners in FE come from a range of complex and varying backgrounds, studying from entry level 1 to level 7 (master's). Figure 12.1 summarises the levels, highlighting academic, vocational and work-based routes to higher education. Generally, FE providers will deliver qualifications from entry level to level 7 in some cases.

Job roles in FE

Staff referred to in FE as Learning Support Services (LSS) can have a range of job titles with various tasks. These complexities, combined with the varying support needs of FE SEND learners make the role of learning support in FE complex, challenging and extremely rewarding.

DOI: 10.4324/9781003261506-13

Level	Qualification / educational route		
8	Doctorate (PhD)		NVQ 8
7	Master's degree (MA)		
6	Bachelor's degree BA or BSc		Degree apprenticeship / NVQ 5, 6, 7
5	Foundation degree FdA or FdSc	Higher National Diploma (HND)	
4		Higher National Certificate (HNC)	Higher apprenticeship / NVQ 4
3	A levels Grades A-E / International Baccalaureate / T Levels	BTEC diploma / BTEC certificate	Advanced apprenticeship / NVQ 3
2	GCSE Grades 4-9 (C,B,A or A*)	BTEC first diploma	Intermediate apprenticeship / NVQ 2
1	GCSE Grades 1-3 (D,E,F or G)	Foundation diploma / entry level qualifications	Traineeship / NVQ1
Entry Levels	Academic route	Vocational route	Applied / work route

Figure 12.1 Summary of academic, vocational and work-based routes to higher education
Adapted from GOV.UK (2021)

There is no standard role, job title or job description for LSS (it varies between provider). However, their commonality is that they directly support individual learners or groups of learners in a classroom or remote setting (Robson, Bailey and Mendick, 2006).

Policy in FE

Policy reform alongside human rights discourse brought positive change for post-16 learners with learning difficulties and disabilities (LDD), enabling them to be included in colleges with their peers (Tomlinson, 2010). All FE learners with SEND are equally encouraged to access and participate in services and education designed to increase their skills for life and work, thus improving their life chances (Peters, 2010). Colleges have seen a marked increase in LSS working in inclusive classrooms supporting learners according to their needs, age and abilities due to these reforms.

As stated in the SEND code of practice, 'colleges should be ambitious for young people with SEN, whatever their needs and whatever their level of study. They should focus on supporting young people so they can progress and reach positive destinations in adult life' (DfE and DoH, 2015, p. 113). SMART targets must be used in settings for children with SEN to ensure that they meet their long-term outcomes.

Increasing motivation through SMART targets

One common argument for implementing SMART targets is increasing learner motivation views, wishes and aspirations. They know what they need to learn and what they need to improve, and achieving the targets marks a natural stage for them, thereby increasing motivation. Therefore, when considering SMART goals with FE SEND learners, the challenge for teachers, SENCOs and LSS is to ensure each section is goal-focused, uses milestones and considers the wellbeing of all involved in the process.

Supporting the transition to FE

All FE colleges, sixth-form colleges, 16–19 academies and independent specialist colleges approved under Section 41 of the CAFA 2014 have a specific statutory duty to co-operate with the LA on arrangements for CYP with SEND (DfE and DoH, 2015).

For all learners, moving to a new learning environment, such as a college, which typically is larger than schools, can be exciting yet also overwhelming (Rice, Frederickson and Seymour, 2011). Figure 12.2 and 12.2a highlights the factors that lead to better, good and poor transition, as identified by teachers, learners and parents during successful transitions into colleges.

Figure 12.3 illustrates how a FE college in the Northeast of England coordinates learners' input in planning their transition. A coordinated approach to transition must consider the young person (YP) holistically and involve all key stakeholders, with the learner being the most important stakeholder. Schools and colleges bring together staff, external partners and stakeholders to build, implement and monitor supportive transition pathways. The model illustrates the contributors to the transition from secondary school to college from an early stage. Note that not all colleges have a qualified SENCO. Therefore, the SEND/LSS manager should be involved in the transition process.

Better Transition
- Information is widely available
- Visits work both ways
- Learners and parent / guardians voices are heard
- Engagement from all stakeholders

Good Transition
- Information is available
- College and school visits
- Learners and parents / guardians have opportunity to speak

Poor Transition
- No visits
- Learners and parents voices are not heard
- Changes without engagement
- No input from stakeholders

Figure 12.2 and *Figure 12.2a* Transition risk indicator
Adapted from Education and Training Foundation (2021)

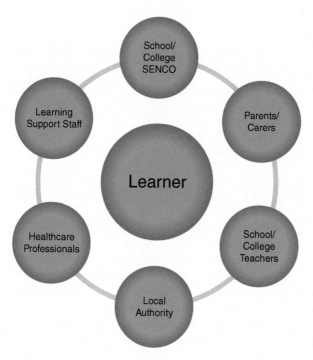

Figure 12.3 Coordinating input

Involving the learner in the transition process

Starting college can be a daunting and distressing time for SEND learners, particularly those with conditions driven by anxiety or who find it challenging to cope in new environments and routines. The transition process from an early stage should focus on settling in quickly and building new foundations. A restorative approach focuses on building relationships with the learner. By adopting this approach, the aim is to create an environment that will help them communicate their thoughts, feelings, concerns and motivations around the transition process. Figure 12.4 details the considerations that should be taken by those involved in the input of transition planning (adapted from Polat et al., 2001). The following transition model provides some helpful considerations to aid a smooth transition.

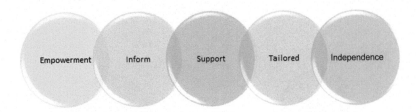

Figure 12.4 Transition considerations

Empowerment

Towards the end of the first term in secondary school, the learner should be supported in making their first steps to progressing onto college. One alternative approach is the booster approach, which emphasises that individuals chart their transitional course and seek guidance as they need it. There is not necessarily a direct visual in-class support, and the responsibility lies with the learner to seek out direct support and resources. An example of this in FE is discrete learning support. The learning support worker provides support from a distance, usually sitting at the back of the class, and supports the teacher with all learners in the class, without drawing direct attention to the SEND learner.

By early planning of the learners' onward transitions from their very first term, looking at the outcomes they want to achieve and the steps all involved need to put in place to make this happen, learners should be encouraged and supported through their future planning as young adults. Caregivers can be an important source of support in preparing learners for the transition.

Inform

Informing the LA of their intentions is a reciprocal duty. Both the LA and FE provider must co-operate to ensure the college can meet the learner's needs. Young people have the right to request that an institution is named in their EHCP. LAs must name that institution in the EHCP. Unless, following consultation with the institution, the LA determines that it is unsuitable for the young person's age, ability, aptitude or SEN, or that to place the young person there would be incompatible with the efficient use of resources or the efficient education of others (DfE and DoH, 2015).

Florian et al. (2000), based on an investigation of 233 special schools' provision for pupils with SEN in England and Wales, argued that those with complex and profound learning difficulties are offered limited choices after their compulsory schooling. Therefore, information, advice and guidance (IAG) are key for all learners transitioning into post-16 studies. This includes discussing which qualification might suit the learners – academic, work-related or specific job-related routes – and thinking about which courses or jobs they might be considering and where this might fit. Their disability should not be a barrier when considering course choice.

'Schools and colleges should raise the career aspirations for their SEN students and broaden their employment horizons' (DfE and DoH, 2015, p. 28).

Suggested material and resources may include transition support booklets for learners, SENCOs/LSS, teachers and parents, and should help inform all those involved in the transition process. IAG practitioners can provide useful support and information around courses and employment options.

Support

It is generally accepted that SEND is 'best met by planned, cross-professional approaches, rather than independent initiatives' (McCartney, 2002. p. 67). The coordinating input (Figure 12.3) of those involved in the learner's care, support and EHC plan must ensure communication is paramount from an early stage. Peer mentors and visits to college should support learners with the transition to FE. It is helpful if they commence at the second term in secondary school (typically January). Regular contact between school and college learning support will also help ensure the learner's needs are in place before they start college. Building relationships before they begin at their new setting is paramount to a successful transition.

Suggested material and resources may include Transition Concern Questionnaires.

Tailored

The transition pathway is not just about supporting learners to reach the next stage of their education but equipping them with the confidence, social and independence skills they need to flourish once they are there. No two transitions are the same, and every learner's pathway is tailored to their particular needs. Careers advice for learners with SEND should be inspirational and aspirational, imaginative, impartial, well-informed and individualised (Brooks, 2018).

Independence

Independence is co-created by both the exiting school and the ongoing college. Schools and colleges must work together to develop life skills, focus on progressing into adulthood both physically and mentally, and prepare for the new college environment. To support the transition to FE, the provider must understand the particular SEN and plans for how the YP will access their new provision. Indeed, the DfE guidance for FE states 'where a student has a learning difficulty or disability that calls for special educational provision, the college must use its best endeavours to put appropriate support in place' (2014, p. 10). Table 12.1 provides key questions to ask the CYP and their caregiver, where appropriate, to co-produce transition arrangements.

Table 12.1 Key questions in preparation for transition to FE

Special considerations and additional arrangements that may be required		
Area	*Key questions*	*Actions*
SEND	What are the YP's strengths, views, wishes and aspirations? What diagnoses does the YP have? Does the YP require an individual health care plan?	
Transport	How will YP get to and from the setting? When/how often will they practise travelling to college? Who will support them with planning and preparing for travel? What contingency plans are in place if problems arise while on transport?	

Special considerations and additional arrangements that may be required

Area	Key questions	Actions
Environment	Will there be any issues with moving around the setting? Will YP need access to quiet spaces? Does YP need adapted provision for break times and/or lunchtimes? Does YP need to sit in a specified place in class? Does the YP have any particular anxieties due to COVID-19 transmission?	
Relationships	What additional support is available to help YP build positive relationships with peers? What additional support is available to help YP build positive relationships with adults?	
Pastoral support	Will there be a designated key person they can talk to if they need to? How will they access additional pastoral support? Is there a quiet place to go to at break and/or lunchtimes, if needed?	
Resources to support enhanced transitions	One-page profile template, photo booklets, checklists, 'my new college' booklet, prompt cards, information cards, social stories and 'my usual week looks like this' timetable.	
Qualifications	What qualifications have the YP already achieved and/or what are they predicted to achieve? Have they been previously assessed for exam access arrangements (e.g., 25% extra time, reader)?	
Independent advice and guidance	Has the YP had recent independent careers advice and guidance?	
Programme of Study	Is the programme of study appropriate for the YP? Is there a requirement for work experience? Will the programme support the YP with entry into work or further/higher education?	

Identify any curriculum adaptations that need to be made

Key support services and resources to signpost for CYP, families and settings

Preparing for the first on-site visit

Through careful planning, most YP with SEND can transition well into FE, particularly when opportunities are provided to visit the site before beginning their programmes of study.

> Schools and colleges should work in partnership to provide opportunities such as taster courses, link programmes and mentoring, which enable young people with SEND to familiarise themselves with the college environment and gain some experience of college life and study.
>
> (DfE, 2014, p. 13)

Table 12.2 shares an example of a transition visit plan for YP with SEND. A completed version is provided for Sophie (Table 12.3).

Table 12.2 Generic transition visit plan

Transition visits

Key considerations pre-on-site visit:

- Many YP may have particular anxieties about COVID-19 transmission
- Ensure you have gathered the information in Table 12.1
- Does the student have any allergies, medical needs, sensory sensitivities, physical support needs, accessibility or language difficulties?
- How will the YP travel to and from the visit? Will they be accompanied?

More than one visit may be required. The number and types of visits planned should be responsive to the particular needs of the YP and family:

- Consider some visits after teaching hours when the setting is empty
- Provide opportunities to meet key staff, including support staff
- Provide opportunities to meet peers in small groups
- Plan time to visit outside spaces
- Plan visits at a social time to review any adjustments that need to be made

Date	Purpose	Outcome	Further visits required?

Case study: Sophie

About Sophie: Sophie had a diagnosis of autism and was transitioning to FE from a small special school based in NE England. She wanted to train to be a chef after doing some work experience in the canteen at her school. Her transition encompassed the following considerations, which fed into her transition support plan.

Table 12.3 Sophie's transition visit plan

Transition visits

Key considerations pre-on-site visit:
- Many YP may have particular anxieties about COVID-19 transmission
- Ensure you have gathered the information in Table 12.1
- Does the student have any allergies, medical needs, sensory sensitivities, physical support needs, accessibility, language difficulties?
- How will the YP travel to and from the visit? Will they be accompanied?

More than one visit may be required. The number and types of visits planned should be responsive to the particular needs of the YP and family:
- Consider some visits after teaching hours when the setting is empty
- Provide opportunities to meet key staff, including support staff
- Provide opportunities to meet peers in small groups
- Plan time to visit outside spaces
- Plan visits at a social time to review any adjustments that need to be made

Date	Purpose	Outcome	Further visits required?
November 2022	Introduction to FE	Provide robust IAG to Sophie on the FE environment, programmes, support and offer. Review EHCP with SENCO and start an early transition. Identify any transport and COVID-19 barriers.	Yes, Sophie's first on-site visit.
January 2023	First on-site visit	Sophie and her parents to visit the college, LSS and curriculum staff, and meet some learners with EHCPs already on programme.	Yes, second college visit.

(Continued)

Table 12.3 (Continued) Sophie's transition visit plan

Easter 2023	Second on-site visit to include participation in learning activities	Sophie to attend the Easter transition programme both with and without parental support. Address any further needs identified.	Yes, Sophie to attend summer school programme.
July 2023	Third on-site visit to include final transition requirements	Sophie to finalise initial support needs in preparation for September start. Teaching staff to begin/review scheme of learning ahead of welcoming Sophie in class.	Electronic support, such as Microsoft Teams, to keep in contact with curriculum and LSS.

Sophie was invited to both the Easter and summer school support sessions. These week-long sessions allow new learners to visit the college and meet staff while being introduced to the environment during quiet periods. Here, Sophie identified what support she would need when studying at college. IAG were also provided to Sophie regarding what programmes were offered and what vocational routes these could lead to.

Sophie and her family were informed of what the local offer was, what support services were at the college and how her EHCP would be updated to include vocational objectives. LSS and student services then worked with Sophie's family to support them in completing applications and providing funding support.

Following several other visits to the college and a visit to her school by LSS, Sophie was enrolled on a full-time level 1 professional cookery programme. This provided Sophie with work experience in college and the college restaurant, and an external work placement in a busy kitchen preparing food.

Sophie was progressing well and hoped to stay in college and move to the level 2 programme in professional cookery. She gained paid employment working on a weekend in the kitchen where she did her work placement.

The previous case study highlights why successful transition is essential, as Ofsted's Moving Forward report (2012) states, 'the provision of specialist impartial careers guidance to learners with high needs was generally weak'. It highlights the low employment rate; only 5.8% of adults known to social services with moderate to severe learning difficulties are in paid employment.

Transition planning as a process

A successful transition depends on many factors, each unique to the individual. Overall, most colleges and schools manage transition arrangements effectively for their learners with additional learning needs, who may need specialist support. In general, staff in schools and colleges ensure that these learners' progression is well-planned from an early stage (Table 12.4). A growing evidence base (Humphrey and Ainscow, 2006; Hughes, Banks and Terras, 2013) indicates that transition can work well for learners with SEND if schools and colleges dedicate time to the appropriate planning and personalised support, as highlighted earlier.

Colleges need to make sure that necessary adaptations or learning aids are in place in good time for the learners to settle into the institution quickly and make good progress in their learning. Nevertheless, weaknesses remain. For example, as Estyn's annual report (2013–2014) identified, transitions for learners between settings and primary schools, primary and secondary schools, and secondary schools and post-16 providers, have been a focus of many reviews, reports and policy initiatives. Yet there are still obstacles to sharing information about CYP. They add there are very few examples of systematic joint planning between providers across the transition points (Estyn, 2015, p. 16).

Table 12.4 illustrates that if planning is treated as a process rather than an event, it can be thought of as a sequence with several stages (or steps), leading to actions that inform the next stage.

Once decisions about a learner's preferred transition have been made, the next step is action planning, which is informed by the SEN code of practice (DfE and DoH, 2015). Action planning is a crucial feature of effective practice because it ensures that decisions can be implemented and progress reviewed. Action planning links SMART targets with actions to realise them, identifies barriers and risks and plans how to minimise or manage them, and incorporates a process of review (for example, to monitor progress and, if necessary, revise the plan).

Table 12.4 Transition planning as a process

- Action planning: Translating choices and decisions into actions
  1 Focusing on the long term (not just the next step)
  2 Coordination between the young person, caregivers and other stakeholders
  3 Flexibility and responsiveness (e.g., as needs or circumstances change)
  4 Monitoring and evaluating the process

Step	Key elements
Step 1: develop an inclusive, person-centred transition planning process	Start early and use your best judgement: there is no right way to structure transition planning Identify who needs to be involved, and when and how to involve them; and build trust
Step 2: enable young people and parents/caregivers to make informed choices about transitions	Put the learner first; focus on their abilities and aspirations while considering others' interests Ensure IAG is accessible, accurate and relevant Consider providing independent advice and support and identify and negotiate between competing interests
Step 3: prepare learners, parents and carers, and education settings for the chosen transition	Share information and knowledge about the young person Ensure young people, parents and carers, and settings are prepared (including identifying and addressing potential barriers to transition) Adapt provision and support, as required, to meet young people's needs and collaborate and exercise systems leadership
Step 4: support learners' progression following transition (including planning for subsequent transitions)	Ensure that assessments are holistic and focused on the learner's academic, personal and social needs Ensure that assessment is an ongoing process – not an event Identify those at risk of disengagement (and act) Ensure effective planning for learners' progression

(Adapted from Holtom et al., 2016)

Preparation for adulthood

SEND reforms enacted through the CAFA (2014) were intended to join up support across education, health and care, from birth to 25. Learners and parents/carers should be fully involved in decisions about their support and what the learner wants to achieve.

The reforms are intended to deliver the following:

* A positive experience of the system for children, young people and families
* Improved outcomes for CYP
* Effective preparation for adulthood

The SEND reforms enabled a new focus on preparing for adulthood – no more falling off the conveyor belt or assuming a lifetime on benefits or social care. One of the more challenging aspects of the reform was the significant culture change for everyone, from parents and young people to LAs and education providers. Caregivers and learners with SEND want preparation for employment, independent living, community participation and best possible health.

> The overwhelming majority of young people with SEN are capable of sustained paid employment with the right preparation and support. All professionals working with them should share that presumption.
>
> (DfE and DoH, 2015, p. 33)

The transition from school to post-16 education and adult life is not a single point in a timeline, but part of the lifelong process of individual development (Szymanski, 1993). Moreover, learners with SEND benefit from multiple vocational experiences, but this must only be embarked upon after a careful assessment of the strengths and needs of the individual and the development of a structured, individualised transition support plan. Nonetheless, transition support plans remain a resource-heavy, complex process that in England would benefit from more funding in research and practice. Thus, the central role of transition planning to empower learners with SEND requires the transition plan to be successful. Most importantly, the learner should have high aspirations, seek advice or advocacy, and be willing to participate in planning for their future.

Chapter summary

* Transition planning for learners with SEND provides an essential individualised set of opportunities for active learning about the self, careers and work.

- Transition planning can provide a structured environment to develop the broad range of life, social and employability skills necessary to transition successfully from school to FE.
- Evidence base highlights the importance of beginning the transition process early through personalised guidance, involving the young person and their caregivers.
- Information should be shared by the current setting with the receiving setting to support the transition.

 Further reading

Addy, T.M., Dube, D. et al. (2021) *What inclusive instructors do: Principles and practices for excellence in college teaching.* London: Disability Rights UK.

Curran, H. (2019) *How to be a brilliant SENCO: Practical strategies for developing and leading inclusive provision (nasen spotlight).*

Goodall, C. (2020) *Understanding the voices and educational experiences of autistic young people: From research to practice (Routledge research in special educational needs).*

Ramshaw, E. (2017) *The post-16 SENCO handbook: An essential guide to policy and practice (nasen spotlight).*

Scanlon, G., Barnes-Holmes, Y. et al. (2019) *Transition for pupils with special educational needs; implications for inclusion policy and practice.*

References

Brooks, H. (2018) *Post-16 choices: The police perspective.* London: Disability Rights UK.

Children and Families Act (CAFA) 2014. Available at: https://www. legislation.gov.uk/ukpga/2014/6/contents/enacted (Accessed: 25 November 2021).

Department for Education (DfE) (2014) *Further education: Guide to the 0 to 25 SEND code of practice.* London: DfE.

DfE and DoH (2015) *Special educational needs and disability code of practice. 0-25 years.* London: DfE.

DfE and Department of Health (DoH) (2015) *Special educational needs and disability code of practice: 0 to 25 years: Statutory guidance for organisations which work with and support children and young people who have special educational needs or disabilities.* London: DfE.

Education and Training Foundation (ETF) (2021) *CfE (Centre for Excellence) SEND blog: Transition to and within further education, a learners and parent's perspective.* Available at: https://www.et-foundation.co.uk/send/cfesend-blog-transition-to-and-within-further-education-a-learners-and-parents-perspective/ (Accessed: 8 November 2021).

Estyn (2015) *The Annual Report of Her Majesty's Chief Inspector of education and training in Wales.* Available at: http://www.estyn.gov.uk/english/annual- report/annual-report-2013-2014/ (Accessed: 8 November 2021).

Florian, L., Dee, L., Byers, R. and Maudslay, L. (2000) 'What happens after the age of 14? Mapping transitions for pupils with profound and complex learning difficulties', *British Journal of Special Education,* 27(3), pp. 124–128.

GOV.UK (2021) *What qualification levels mean.* Available at: https://www.gov.uk/what-different-qualification-levels-mean/list-of-qualification-levels (Accessed: 21 November 2021).

Holtom, D., Lloyd-Jones, S., Bowen, R. and Watkins, J. (2016) *Special educational needs transition from school to further learning.* Cardiff: Welsh Government.

Hughes, L.A., Banks, P. and Terras, M.M. (2013) 'Secondary school transition for children with special educational needs: A literature review', *Support for Learning,* 28(1), pp. 24–34.

Humphrey, N. and Ainscow, M. (2006) 'Transition club: Facilitating learning, participation and psychological adjustment during the transition to secondary school', *European Journal of Psychology of Education,* 21, pp. 319–331.

McCartney, E. (2002) 'Cross-sector working: Speech and language therapists in education', *Journal of Management in Medicine*, 16(1), pp. 67–77. doi: 10.1108/02689230210428634.

Ofsted (2012) *Moving English forward: Action to raise standards in English*. London: Ofsted.

Peters, S.J. (2010) 'The heterodoxy of student voice: Challenges to identity in the sociology of disability and education', *British Journal of Sociology of Education*, 31(5), pp. 591–602.

Polat, F., Kalambouka, A., Boyle, W.F. and Nelson, N. (2001) *Post-16 transitions of pupils with special educational needs*. London: DfES.

Rice, F., Frederickson, N. and Seymour, J. (2011) 'Assessing pupil concerns about transition to secondary school', *British Journal of Educational Psychology*, 81, pp. 244–263.

Robson, J., Bailey, B. and Mendick, H. (2006) *An investigation into the roles of learning support workers*. London: Learning and Skills Network.

Szymanski, E.M. (1993) 'Career development, school to work transition and diversity: An ecological approach', in *Transition from school to work: New opportunities for adolescents*, edited by F.R. Rusch and J. Chadsey-Rusche. Pacific Grove, CA: Brooks/Cole.

Tomlinson, S. (2010) 'A tribute to Len Barton', *British Journal of Sociology of Education*, 31(5), pp. 537–546.

Index

Page numbers in *italics* indicate a figure and page numbers in **bold** indicate a table on the corresponding page.